Shake Off the Sugar Cookbook

Not all carbs are created equal!

By Lynn Stephens

Most of the graphics are licensed by ArtToday.com

The information in this book is not intended to give or replace medical advice.

"Shake Off the Sugar Cookbook," by Lynn Stephens. ISBN 1-58939-303-1.

Published 2002 by Virtualbookworm.com Publishing Inc., P.O. Box 9949, College Station, TX, 77842, US. ©2003 by Lynn Stephens. All rights reserved. No part of this publication may be reproduced, stored in a retrieval system, or transmitted in any form or by any means, electronic, mechanical, recording or otherwise, without the prior written permission of Lynn Stephens.

Manufactured in the United States of America.

Table Of Contents

You Can Shake Off the Sugar

Calories don't count. Fat doesn't lead to flab - but eating the wrong carbohydrates does. Many of us have tried to control our weight and improve our health by drastically reducing fat in our diet. Unfortunately, these changes have not worked. Instead, our society has seen an increase in obesity and higher tendencies toward diabetes and heart disease. Today, there are more overweight people in the United States than there are people of a healthy weight.

More experts are finally recognizing the value of a diet with a higher percentage of protein and one that is low glycemic in nature. A low glycemic diet is comprised of foods that do not trigger sudden surges in blood sugar. Carbohydrates should be included in your food choices, along with protein and a certain amount of healthy fat. The trick is in choosing carbohydrates that have a low glycemic value. These carbohydrates deliver necessary dietary fiber and more nutrients than their starchy relatives. They give us a steady supply of energy without excess calories being stored as fat.

When your body has to produce large amounts of insulin to clean up excess carbohydrates, insulin stores those carbohydrates as fat. A low glycemic diet works because the pancreas no longer has to produce excessive amounts of insulin. It has been found that a diet that brings insulin under control can be a powerful prevention for a number of lifestyle illnesses. Best of all, a low glycemic diet is a healthy way to bring your weight under control.

Understanding the effects of insulin will completely change the way you make food choices. But getting started can be a real problem. Shopping for the right foods is time consuming until you get into the swing of making different choices for your diet. It took a bit of research for me to make the changes for my family, not to mention lots of label reading.

At the time we started a low glycemic diet, I searched, but I could not find one recipe book that was devoted to low glycemic recipes. So I started my own. My recipes will be helpful to everyone who has chosen to take control of your own weight and also to those who need to watch their triglycerides, cholesterol and blood sugar. I found that the hardest part in making this change was in knowing where to start. This book is designed to help you do just that.

Shake Off the Sugar includes recipes, shopping tips, nutritional information, and strategies for staying on a low glycemic diet. I would like to share what I have learned to help you control your weight and improve your overall health.

The only thing you need is commitment to your own well being and a bit of education so that you can be in control - not your food cravings. Eating a low glycemic diet will help you to lose excess weight at a slow and steady pace. You really can eat well, enjoy your food, become trim, and feel great. Take the first step and shake off your sugar habit!

A Low Glycemic Diet -Eat for Your Health

In removing fat from so many foods, something far worse has often been substituted. When fat is removed from foods and recipes, flavor and texture are lost. In order to compensate for that loss, the food industry often substitutes sugars and starches. It seems like a good idea, but it is not. The wrong carbohydrates do more harm to your body than do fats.

Of course, everyone should trim excess fat from meats and be moderate in the use of fat. Unfortunately, we have been frightened into avoiding all fats. In moderation, the right fats are actually needed by your body. Even your brain functions better with appropriate amounts of healthy fat. Understanding the way your body utilizes food will explain why.

Conventional wisdom says that fat is converted to fat and sugars and starches are converted to energy. But that is not how your body actually works. The actual mechanism that causes your body to store food as fat is a powerful hormone. That hormone is insulin. As long as insulin is kept at low to moderate levels, your body will work efficiently and will not store food as excessive fat.

Insulin is essential to each of us. Simply put, insulin controls the amount of blood sugar in our bodies. When eaten, foods are broken down into simple sugars (glucose). When food is rapidly broken down and converted to sugar, it will rapidly raise your blood sugar. Your body then must manufacture enough insulin to carry the glucose to the cells. The more glucose is released, the more insulin your body manufactures. The more insulin your body manufactures, the more food is stored as fat. After all, your body can only use so much glucose as energy at any time.

If you want to control your weight, it is essential to control your blood sugar. Controlling food choices can easily do this. The surprising news is that some of the foods that are low fat actually trigger terrible surges in glucose levels. This causes your pancreas to shoot insulin into your system to bring down the blood sugar. At the same time, the high levels of insulin sweep excess sugar into your adipose (fat) cells. In other words, your cells gobble the excess sugars as fat because there is so much excess insulin. When this happens often enough, pounds pile on.

Eating foods that do not raise your blood sugar will not cause your body to store the food as excess fat. Enough insulin is not released at one time to do that job. How wonderful! Control of body fat! Not only that, but eating small, low-glycemic meals throughout the day nourishes your muscles and promotes a steady supply of energy.

Insulin stimulates your body to produce cholesterol. As proof of this, doctors have noted that their diabetic patients who must rely on insulin injections have higher levels of cholesterol than do the average population. (Steward, et.al., 1995) A low glycemic diet usually helps to lower cholesterol levels. It stands to reason that it is wise to control surges of insulin in your body.

Diabetes is another major health concern in today's society. Studies have shown that a direct relationship exists between the growth of sugar and carbohydrate consumption and the growth in the number of people who develop diabetes. For example, American Indians began to develop diabetes at a much higher rate after they made the change from maize to hybrid corn. The hybridized corn we eat today has a much higher proportion of carbohydrates to protein and fiber and thus has a higher glycemic value.

For thousands of years, people primarily ate protein, fruit, vegetables, nuts, and berries. They did not have high carbohydrate diets. Because of this, diabetes was not the problem it is today. As table sugar and refined grains became more available, the rate of diabetes increased. The average American today consumes about 120 pounds of sugar each year. At the beginning of the 19th century, Europeans were consuming only seven pounds per year. It is believed that not only diabetes, but also other twentieth-century diseases such as heart disease and cancer are directly related to such changes in our diets.

Most of us have experienced eating binges. The more your insulin is overly stimulated, the more likely you are to have eating binges. These binges are caused by a natural chemical reaction that takes place in the human body. A sudden drop in sugar levels and a need for energy follows a sugar-high in the body. This causes more hunger and more binging, for the body cannot convert fat to sugar as efficiently as it converts sugar to fat. What a great method for storing fat in your body! Who needs that? Isn't it nice that regulating blood sugar can often control eating binges.

High and low swings in the blood sugar can cause mood swings, in addition to weight gain and eating binges. Women who suffer with PMS often suffer from insulin that has been elevated by estrogen. There is a helpful way to control the problem of mood swings associated with PMS. Changing your diet to one made up of foods which moderate the blood sugar is far better for your health, both physically and mentally.

Your mind itself needs a steady, controlled supply of food. If your sugar level drops suddenly after eating the wrong carbohydrate, the body then must find sugars to feed the organs and brain. It doesn't take the sugars from the fat cells. Instead, it first breaks down protein (muscle) to form the needed energy to maintain the functioning of your body. Therefore, a low glycemic diet should improve your mental focus. Your body will not have to work as hard to maintain a steady flow of energy to the brain when you are eating correctly.

It is also important to know that pancreatic enzymes are vital in helping your body fight disease. Studies suggest that excessive amounts of animal protein, over time, can lead to pancreatic deterioration; but, too much of the wrong carbohydrates can lead to diabetes. Try to find the balance between protein and carbohydrates. Your body needs both. The foods you choose have a tremendous impact on your future health.

In addition to insulin, your pancreas produces glucagon. Its function is the opposite of insulin; glucagon works to prevent your blood sugar from falling too low. Glucagon helps your body to burn the fat that is stored. When insulin is controlled by eating low glycemic foods, your pancreas can produce higher levels of glucagon, which then is free to metabolize excess fat.

Choosing a low glycemic diet is a way of eating that works only if you are committed. Cheating can cause weight gain, not weight loss. But making the change is worth the effort. Be patient. Remember you are human and may stray from the plan. If you do stray, just start fresh at the next meal. The more you practice this new way of choosing food, the easier it becomes.

You may also experience weight fluctuations that are part of your natural hormonal rhythms. Remember that it is normal to hit plateaus, as well. Persevere. Do not give up! Over time, you will be rewarded. This is not an overnight way to weight loss, but a change of life-style, a change that will lead you to well-being, restored energy, and a body that is the size it was meant to be.

Fabulous Fats

Fat, in and of itself, will not make anyone gain weight. Fat is an essential part of a healthy diet. The fatty acids that your body needs most are called essential fatty acids (EFA): omega-3 fatty acids and linoleic acid. These fats are needed by your brain and heart and also affect depression. Your body needs both types of fats. It cannot make its own, but uses these fatty acids to make many others that we also must have.

The omega-3s are found in fatty fish, such as mackerel, salmon, bluefish, rainbow trout, anchovies, sardines, and flaxseed oil. Be aware: too much fish oil or flaxseed oil can increase the need for vitamin E; do take supplements. One or two servings per week of omega-3 are more than sufficient.

Linoleic acid can be found in the seed oils: safflower, sunflower, sesame, flax, peanut, evening primrose, canola, and soybean. This type of oil is best if it is cold-pressed. Look for the processing method on the label. Heat destroys nutrients in these oils. You need linoleic acid in your diet because the human body cannot manufacture them. Your body needs more omega-3 than linoleic acid. Do use the seed oils in salad dressings and in other dishes where the oil will not receive further cooking. These oils can become rancid and are best stored in the refrigerator. They should be purchased in small amounts so that the goodness of the oil will not begin to break down before you use it. I purchase the oils that have been preserved with vitamin E, which extends the shelf life of the oil.

Essential fatty acids (EFAs) shorten the recovery time from fatigue and help to prevent the damage that may be caused by hard fats. EFAs help to lower cholesterol and blood pressure. They promote healthy skin and tissue and help the immune system, as well. Unlike hard fats, which slow down your metabolism, EFAs actually help our bodies to run faster.

Moderate amounts of fat also slow down the progression of food to your lower intestine, thus helping you to feel full. If you do not consume enough fat, you will feel hungry more quickly, causing you to increase your total intake of carbohydrates, and you know what eating the wrong carbohydrates does!

I was surprised to find that unrefined coconut oil is not bad for you, but the processed kind is. If you choose to use unrefined coconut oil for cooking, you should be able to find it or order it at your health food store. Unrefined coconut oil is white, not yellow. Olive oil is also a good choice for cooking, but, again, choose the unrefined oils. Unrefined olive oil is labeled as extra virgin and is green in color. People who live in countries that rely heavily on these two oils in their unrefined state have a lower incidence of heart disease. Unrefined oils are often labeled as cold-pressed. Canola oil is fine for occasional cooking when you need an oil with a light taste, but it is best not to consume it on a regular basis.

When cooking with fats, always use the lowest possible temperature. When frying with oil, never allow the oil to get so hot that it smokes. Overheating the oil changes the molecular structure of the oil, causing it to loose its health benefits. Butter holds up better that most other fats at high temperatures and is fine to use.

Avoid hydrogenated shortenings (hardened oils) whenever possible. They really are bad for your health, for they contain trans-fatty acids, which have been linked to heart disease. Butter is acceptable in moderation and is actually a healthier choice than most margarine. Isn't that lovely?

The Glycemic Index

One of the best tools for planning a carbohydrate-controlled diet is called the glycemic index. This index was first devised in 1981. It was created in Canada by Dr. David Jenkins as a way to help diabetics choose food. At the time it was controversial, but has now become a clinically proven tool for choosing foods that control blood sugar. Scientists now understand that all carbohydrates are not the same and that our bodies do not treat them in the same manner. For example, one-half cup of mashed potatoes can send your insulin levels surging, but one-half cup of lentils has very little effect on your glucose levels.

The index assigns values to foods according to how quickly the foods release sugar into the body. Some of the worst offenders will probably surprise you: white potatoes, corn, carrots, white rice and anything made with refined grains. Corn and white potatoes cause your blood sugar to spike worse than table sugar! I have compiled several glycemic indexes into one. You can find the list on the following pages. You will find this index to be a terrific key for opening the door to a low glycemic life-style.

The recipes in this book were created with this index in mind. Any glycemic value over 50 (some say 60) is considered to be high (one-half the value of glucose). A number of factors can affect the glycemic value of food. Fiber and fat tend to lower the glycemic value when combined with a recipe or a meal, so the glycemic value of any given recipe is probably less than any one ingredient. Making acidic additions like vinegar and lemon juice can also lower the GI of a food.

Not everyone will react in the same way to given foods. The glycemic index is a general guideline, taken by testing a number of people eating the same amount (one-half cup servings) of the same foods. One thing that should be noted is that portion size does matter. If the food amount is increased, so is the elevation in blood sugar and therefore insulin. The Glycemic Index is an average taken from a number of people consuming the same food. Each person is different. If you find a particular food that causes you to have carbohydrate cravings or causes you to gain weight, then you are probably sensitive to that food. It is best to leave foods that cause you problems completely alone.

tofu frozen dessert	115
Jasmine rice	109
maltose	105
dates	103
glucose	100
glutinous white rice	98
russet potatoes	98
puffed rice	95
white potatoes	70-90
white bread	95
parsnips	95
honey	90
carrots	85
instant potatoes	80
tapioca	80
jelly beans (5)	80
vanilla wafers (6)	77
corn/cornflakes	70-85
refined sugar	75
millet	75
pumpkin	75
corn tortilla	72
rutabaga	71
corn chips	71
whole wheat bread	70
beets	70
white rice	70
shredded wheat	70
Mars Bar	68
Swiss Museli	67
refined pasta	65
raisins	65
figs	61
bananas	60
pastry	59
basmati white rice	58
new potatoes	58
brown rice	55
green peas	51
potato chips	51
whole rice	50
whole grain bread	40-50
grapes	50
sweet potatoes	50
pineapple juice	48
wheat grains	45
whole grain pasta	45
sponge cake	45
pears	45
orange juice	45

All Bran	42
whole grain rye	42
apple juice	40
oranges	40
apples	40
oatmeal (not instant)	40
tomatoes	38
tomato juice	37
ice cream	36
chick peas	36
lima beans	36
quinoa (cooked)	35
milk, yogurt	35
dried apricots	35
All Bran (extra fiber)	33
beans & peas	30-40
peaches	30
kidney beans	29
lentils	29
sausages	28
grapefruit	26
plums	25
cherries	23
dark chocolate (70% cocoa)	22
fructose	20
walnuts	15
soybeans	15
peanuts	10
mushrooms	10
tomatoes	10
onion	10
green vegetables	0-15
prickly pear	7

Fiber Facts

Fiber is an important part of a low glycemic diet. Fiber is vital and is found in many natural foods. It is essential for a healthy digestive system. Dietary fiber is known to prevent colon cancer, hemorrhoids, diverticulitis, and help to reduce cholesterol. Try to make it a habit to read food labels. Then, choose foods that provide more dietary fiber. They are by their nature lower in glycemic value.

Everyone needs to consume a variety of fibers. Some are soluble and some are insoluble. Soluble fibers are found in dried beans, fruits and to a lesser degree, in vegetables. Soluble fibers dissolve when digested or cooked. Each type of fiber serves its own unique function in your digestive system. Soluble fiber tends to reduce blood sugar and blood fat levels.

Insoluble fiber is found in grains, fruits, and vegetables. Insoluble fibers are those that are composed of cellulose and hemicellulose. These fibers make up the cell walls of the plant.

High fiber foods are often chewy. This helps to clean your teeth of bacteria and plaque. Chewing stimulates the base of the teeth and gums, which increases the flow of blood to the inside of your mouth. This then carries nutrients and antibodies to the linings of your mouth, promoting their general health.

As a note of caution, chewy high fiber foods should probably not be fed to children under the age of five years. Young children can get these foods stuck in their throat, for they do not chew their foods well. After the age of five, high fiber foods should be added to their diet for a life of healthy eating.

If that is not enough, fiber helps to control excess stomach acid. Judging by the advertisements in this country, this is a major concern. Dietary fiber regulates the hormones that produce acid and pepsin.

Even better, having enough fiber in your diet can go a long way toward helping with weight control. Fiber stays in your stomach longer during the digestive process, slowing down the absorption of sugars and starches. Thus, it is an important part of regulating your blood sugar. After a high fiber meal, sugars and starches are digested more slowly. This slow breakdown of food allows the pancreas to produce a smaller amount of insulin over a longer period of time. The result is a steady supply of energy over that longer time period.

Studies have shown that 15 grams of dietary fiber, eaten daily for four months, led to a reduction of 5% to 10% in body weight. However, nutritionists suggest that it is desirable for adults to consume 25 to 30 grams of fiber per day.

Your digestive system must adjust when you change the way you eat. Give yourself a few weeks for the changes to settle down. It helps to keep *Beano* (available in grocery and drug stores) on hand when eating gas-producing foods, such as dried beans and broccoli. Acidophilus and other probiotic tablets are also a wonderful and inexpensive help if you have any food intolerances. This adds back the beneficial bacteria that your system may have lost through taking antibiotic

Following is a dietary fiber index for you to use. The more you know, the better you can eat for your health!

Dietary Fiber Index
All values are for cooked food unless otherwise indicated.

Fiber value (In grams)

Almonds (slivered, dried, 1cup) 14.7
Apple
1 small, without skin 2.0
1 small, with skin 3.0
Applesauce (1 cup) 4.0
Apricots (2-3 medium) 2.1
Artichoke (1 large) 3.0
Artichoke hearts (1/2 cup) 4.5
Asparagus (4 spears, ½" base) 1.3
Avocado (1 whole) 4.7
Bacon 0
Banana (6") 1.75
Barley, pearl, raw (1/2 cup) 6.5
Beans, baked (1/2 cup) 7.5
Beans, garbanzo (1/2 cup) 4.5
Beans, green (1/2 cup 3.2
Beans, kidney (1/2 cup) 10.0
Beans, lima (1/2 cup) 5.1
Beans, navy (1/2 cup) 8.3
Beans, pinto (1/2 cup) 8.2
Beans, sprouts (1 cup) 4.0
Beer... 0
Beets (1 cup) 2.8
Blackberries (1/2 cup) 3.6
Blackeyed Peas (1/2 cup) 7.2
Blueberries (1/2 cup) 1.7
Bran, oat (1/2 cup) 10.5
Bran, wheat (1/2 cup) 15.5
Brazil nuts (1/3 cup) 9.0
Broccoli (1/2 cup) 2.9
Brussels sprouts (9) 4.2
Buckwheat or kasha (1/2 cup) 9.6
Bulgar (1/2 cup)... 4.8
Cabbage, chopped (1/2 cup)... 2.07
Cantalope (1 whole).. 4.0
Carrots (1/2 cup) 2.78
Cauliflower (1/2 cup) 2.0
Celery (1 large stalk).. 0.9
Cheese, cheddar.. 0
Cheese, cottage 0
Cherries (1/2 cup) 1.7
Chocolate 0
Coconut, shredded (1 cup).. 7.2
Corn (1/2 cup) 3.0
Cornmeal, stone ground (1/2 cup) 6.0
Cranberries, raw (1/2 cup) 2.1
Cucumber (1 medium) 0.4
Currants, dried (1/2 cup) 4.3
Custard.. 0
Dates, chopped (1/2 cup).. 7.5
Doughnuts 0
Eggplant, chopped (1/2 cup) 2.5
Eggs 0

Figs, dried & chopped (1/2 cup)... 14.5
Fish.. 0
Flour, buckwheat (1 cup)... 7.0
Flour, kamut (1 cup).. 16.0
Flour, rye, dark (1 cup).. 12.0
Flour, rye, light (1 cup).. 3.4
Flour, spelt (1 cup).. 20.0
Flour, white, all purpose (1 cup)... 3.4
Flour, whole wheat (1 cup).. 13.0
Grapefruit (1/2 medium)... 0.6
Grapes, green (1/2 cup)... 0.9
Honey.. 0
Honeydew melon (1/4 small)... 0.9
Ice Cream... 0
Jello.. 0
Kale (1/2 cup)... 1.4
Leeks (1/2 cup raw).. 0.9
Lentils (1/2 cup, cooked)... 7.8
Lettuce, leaf (1/2 cup, shredded)...................................... 0.35
Lettuce, romaine (1/2 cup, shredded)................................ 0.7
Macaroni, white flour (1/2 cup).. 0.15
Mango (1/2 medium)... 1.5
Masa (1/2 cup)... 5.5
Mayonnaise.. 0
Meat... 0
Milk.. 0
Mincemeat (1/2 cup)... 3.3
Mushrooms (1/2 cup, raw)... 0.4
Nectarine (1 medium)... 1.2
Noodles, whole wheat (1/2 cup)... 3.8
Oatmeal (1/2 cup dry)... 4.0
Okra (1/2 cup, sliced).. 1.3
Olives (10 medium)... 0
Onion (2.25")... 2.1
Orange (2.25")... 3.6
Orange juice.. 0
Parsnips (1/2 cup)... 3.3
Pasta, plain (1 cup).. 2.4
Pasta, whole wheat (1 cup)... 6.3
Peach (1 medium).. 1.4
Peach (flesh & skin)... 2.28
Peanut butter (1/2 cup).. 7.6
Peanut butter (1 tablespoon) 1.0
Peanuts (1/2 cup)... 8.1
Pear (1 medium) 4.6
Peas, green (1/2 cup).. 3.5
Pecan halves (1/2 cup).. 2.9
Pepper, green (1 large).. 0.9
Pickles(1 large or 16 bread & butter) 1.7
Pineapple, diced (1/2 cup).. 0.7
Pineapple, crushed (1/2 cup)... 0.8
Plum, damson (1 medium).. 2.1
Potato, white (2.25" diameter).. 2.1
Potato chips (1 ounce) 1.0
Preserves, strawberry (1 tbsp)... 2.2
Prunes, dried (8 large)... 16.1
Pumpkin, canned (1 cup) 1.0
Radish (1 medium).. 0.1

Raisins, (1/2 cup) 5.4
Raspberries (1/2 cup).. 6.4
Rhubarb, diced (1/2 cup)... 1.3
Rice, brown (1/2 cup) 4.2
Rice, white (1/2 cup) 0.8
Rice, wild (1/4 cup, raw)... 2.0
Sauerkraut (1/2 cup) 2.3
Shrimp 0
Soybeans (1/2 cup) 9.6
Spaghetti, white (1/2 cup) 0.15
Spinach (1/2 cup, raw) 0.8
Spinach, cooked (1/2 cup) 0.0
Squash, butternut (1/2 cup baked)........................... 2.9
Squash, summer (1/2 cup)....................................... 1.3
Strawberries (1/2 cup)... 1.7
Sweet potato, cooked (1/2 cup) 4.1
Tangerine (1 large)... 1.9
Tapioca.. 0
Tomato (1 small) 1.5
Tomato juice... 0
Turnips, chopped (1/2 cup) 1.8
Walnut halves (1/2 cup) 2.6
Zucchini, sliced (1/2 cup) 1.3

Sugar & Sweeteners

Sweeteners have practically no nutritive value, but everyone enjoys an occasional touch of sweetness in their diets. Choosing a healthy and safe sweetener can be confusing. Use this little primer to help you make choices for your low carb lifestyle.

Sugars

Sucrose (table sugar): Sucrose is usually made from sugar beets or sugar cane. It is useful for baking, not only for its flavor, but also for the texture it imparts to baked foods. Not only does sucrose taste good, but it gives you quick energy. However, there is an enormous downside to that sudden surge of energy. When it is gone, your body craves another "hit" of sugar to maintain the energy. Too much sucrose consumption, just like too much of any of the high-glycemic carbohydrates, leads to excessive insulin surges, which in turn causes the excess carbs to be stored in your fat cells. Because sucrose is a high-glycemic sugar, it is a good idea to substitute other sweeteners. When you are reading labels for sugar content, here are some other forms of sucrose to avoid: raw sugar, brown sugar, turbinado, invert sugar, confectioner's sugar, cane sugar, crystallized cane juice.

High Fructose Corn Syrup: This sweetener is manufactured from cornstarch and has a high glycemic value, that is, it causes your insulin to surge. There is some controversy as to the safety of consuming large amounts of this sweetener over time. High fructose corn syrup is found in numerous products and is not the same as a product that contains only fructose, which is a low-glycemic sweetener.

Fructose: Fructose, also known as fruit sugar, is sweeter than table sugar. Use about one-third less when substituting it for table sugar. Not only do you use less of this sweetener, but it has another advantage. Its glycemic value is 20 (with glucose at 100), very low. Fructose metabolizes at a slow rate, helping to control insulin surges. It is recommended for diabetics and others seeking to control their carbs. Whey Low D is a newly developed product that adds lactose to their fructose, causing an even lower glycemic response than fructose alone. It should be noted that there is concern that excessive use of fructose (more than 20% of your total energy intake) may lead to elevated triglycerides. So, don't go crazy with sweetener. Like all sweeteners, use it in moderation.

Dextrose or Glucose: Glucose has a higher glycemic value than table sugar. On many glycemic indexes, glucose is used as the benchmark for "100". It can also be called corn sugar. Avoid this sugar to control your carbs (and your insulin).

Lactose: Also known as milk sugar, lactose falls about halfway between sucrose and fructose on the glycemic index. It is made from whey and skim milk and is used largely by the pharmaceutical industry.

Honey: Honey is an invert sugar, formed by an enzyme from nectar. It is a combination of fructose, sucrose, glucose, and maltose and is not a low-glycemic sweetener. Honey contains only trace amounts of minerals and vitamins.

Polyols: Also known as sugar alcohols, polyols are found naturally in fruits, but also are manufactured commercially. Xylitol has the same sweetness as sucrose; sorbitol, maltitol, and mannitol as half as sweet as table sugar. Sugar alcohols are useful for diabetics and those who are controlling their insulin because of their low glycemic response. These sugar alcohols are found in a number of "sugar free" products. Their main drawback is that they can have a laxative effect in some people. Exercise caution when trying these products until you see how your own body reacts.

Alternative Sweeteners

Acesulfame potassium (K): Useful for diabetics and more than 200 times sweeter than table sugar, acesulfame K holds up well under the heat of cooking and baking. Its brand name is Sunett. The body cannot metabolize this sweetener, and is excreted in the urine. By itself it can leave a slight aftertaste and has a nice synergistic sweetening effect when combined with other sweeteners. You can find this sweetener under the brand, DiabetiSweet, where it is combined with Isomalt, making it a nice choice for cooking and baking. Acesulfame K is found in numerous products. It has a long shelf life. This sweetener can be substituted for Splenda in the recipes in this book.

Agave Nectar: Also labeled as agave syrup, this sweeter has been used for generations to produce tequila. It is more than 90% fructose and is very low on the glycemic index. When substituting this natural form of fructose for table sugar, use about 30% less. It can be substituted one for one for fructose. This is one of my favorite sweeteners for cooking and baking. It is especially nice to add a small amount of agave when cooking with Splenda to offset some of Splenda's aftertaste and to improve texture. It is a very helpful choice for a controlled carb diet.

Aspartame: Also about 200 times sweeter than sugar, there is a great deal of controversy over the safety of this sweetener. It is made from two amino acids, aspartic acid and phenylalanine. Aspartame, also marketed under the names Nutrasweet and Equal, is found in a wide variety of prepared products. This sweetener does break down when heated and is not useful for cooking or adding to hot beverages.

Maltitol: Unlike many sweeteners, maltitol does not promote tooth decay. This sugar alcohol has a taste and sweetness similar to table sugar. It does not raise glucose, therefore insulin, levels and is useful for diabetics and low-carbers. Because of its high melting point and stability, it is a particularly helpful choice when making candies. It can also give a creamy texture to foods. Like all sugar alcohols, maltitol can have a laxative effect in some individuals.

Saccharine: This sweetener has been around for close to one hundred years and is 200 times sweeter than table sugar. It is produced from a substance found in grapes. The human body cannot break it down, so it does not produce an insulin response. It is often found in soft drinks and in sweetener like Sweet 'N Low. It can be useful in recipes like salad dressings and punch, which do not depend on the volume and texture provided by normal sugars.

Sorbitol: This sugar alcohol is found in a number of products, especially those that tend to become dry or hardened, like candies and confectionaries. Like other sugar alcohols, it does not contribute to tooth decay. Sorbitol is often used in "reduced calorie" and "light" products. Excess consumption may have a laxative effect.

Stevia: Although not approved as a sweetener by the FDA, stevia has been safely used in Japan for the purpose of sweetening for about 25 years. It has only been approved as a food additive in the United States. Stevia products are not standardized, and not all are of the same quality. The pure white powdered extract has the least aftertaste. When using stevia, combining it with at least one other sweetener for better results. Stevia is stable to 400 degrees F, so it holds up well when cooking. However, it will not add texture to baked goods.

Sucralose: Sold under the brand name of Splenda, sucralose is useful as a one to one substitute for table sugar. It is stable when heated and does not break down in cooking. However, I feel you do lose a little of the texture in some baked goods. For some, it also has a slight aftertaste. Because of this, I often substitute a small part of the Splenda with fructose, agave, or Whey Low D. Sucralose does not promote tooth decay. Unless otherwise indicated, the Splenda in the recipes in this book refer to the pourable kind that measures like table sugar.

Powerful Pointers for Controlling Blood Sugar

1. Onions - Throughout history, onions have been prescribed for diabetes. Cooked or raw, the more onions (or onion juice) that are eaten, the lower the blood sugar. Since you cannot have fries, have a small order of onion rings (real ones, not the fast food kind that does not really have onions) when eating out. But, be moderate in doing this because restaurants often do not use healthy oils for cooking.

2. Broccoli - Rich in chromium, broccoli is a wonderful blood sugar regulator. Not only can it lower elevated blood sugar, but it can raise glucose that has dropped too low. One cup of broccoli soup contains 22 micrograms of chromium - ten times more than any other food studied.

3. Other chromium rich foods - Barley, whole grains, nuts, rhubarbs, prunes, peanut butter, mushrooms, liver, cheese and oysters. Enjoy!

4. Curry - Made with fenugreek seeds, this spice has been used in the Middle East and India to help control diabetes. Recent research has supported the insulin controlling influence of this spice. It also seems to lower cholesterol.

5. Cinnamon - Spice up the pumpkin and sweet potatoes. Even in small amounts, it has been found to be effective. Other spices that might help: cloves, tumeric, and bay leaves.

6. Foods high in soluble fiber – Foods like dried beans, fruits and vegetables, not only control insulin activity, but also help to control cholesterol. Try to eat at least 6 grams of soluble fiber per day.

7. Sweet potatoes - For breakfast, lunch, dinner, or snacks (no sugar needed), sweet potatoes deliver energy to your system at a slow, continuous pace, keeping the insulin from spiking to fat-storing levels.

8. Monounsaturated fats are best - These include nuts, avocados, olive and canola oils.

9. Fructose - This sugar can often be used to replace table sugar, but it is 70% sweeter. Use about one-third less. Research has shown that moderate consumption of fructose tends to lead to lower food consumption. Fructose helps to keep blood sugar at a desirable level for a longer period of time. Agave syrup, usually available in health food stores, is a more natural form of fructose and is thought to be a safer choice than crystalline fructose. Fructose-based desserts are best eaten on an empty stomach, or following a small, low-glycemic meal, when your blood sugar is not overly elevated from a large meal.

10. Ingesting protein without carbohydrates can raise your blood sugar. Be sure to eat a small piece of whole grain bread or low glycemic vegetables with your meat! And remember, protein gives long-lasting energy.

11. **Green tea** has been shown to control excess blood sugar. The Chinese and Japanese have used this tea for centuries for their health. Substances (bioflavonoids and polyphenols) in this tea are also thought to have a beneficial effect on lowering high cholesterol and preventing cancer. Today there are wonderful flavored green teas on the market.

12. Adding acid to food lowers the glycemic level of that food. Do prepare your dishes with vinegars, citrus juices and other acidic additions. Some delightful vinegars are available that can jazz up a lifeless dish.

Making the Most of Dining
You do not have to suffer!

Restaurants are usually willing to make substitutions in order to accommodate special needs. So often, potatoes, pasta, corn, or carrots accompany entrees. Ask for extra broccoli or other green vegetables in place of these higher glycemic foods. Broccoli actually helps to regulate blood sugar levels. Whenever possible, choose leafy green salads and skip the iceberg lettuce. Listed below are some suggested substitutions for specific types of restaurants.

American - For appetizers, order fried cheese, bean cakes, even onion blossoms and share. Do not eat the whole thing yourself. French onion soup is a good starter to control your insulin. Grilled Caesar salads are almost always a safe choice. Order sandwiches on whole grain bread. You may have to ask that hamburgers be served on whatever whole grain bread the restaurant has on hand. Otherwise, order the burger without the bread. A hamburger steak with your choice of toppings is quite tasty, even without the bun. Skip the fries. If you absolutely must have dessert, a <u>small</u> scoop of real (never low-fat) or sugar-free ice cream is acceptable. The fat in the ice cream actually acts to lower the glycemic value, but you will still be consuming too much sugar with larger portions.

Italian - Try to choose those restaurants that offer vegetable side dishes as well as pasta. Ignore the bread (at the very least, have only one piece <u>with</u> butter). Enjoy your salad, but not too many carrots. Try to choose entrees that do not require pasta, but if you must have pasta, eat only half the amount you would normally eat (no more than one-half cup). It is better to have dishes that are protein based, such as Veal Marsala or Eggplant Parmesan. If the restaurant has a whole grain pizza crust, go for that! For dessert, have cheese with red wine or a nice cappuccino.

Mexican- Skip the corn chips and order fried stuffed jalapenos. Ask for extra beans in place of rice or corn. And do have sour cream, cheese and guacamole. The fat in avocado is highly nutritious and is one of those fats that act to speed up your metabolism. What could be better?

Asian - If you must have rice, have only a small amount of fried rice - no more than one-half cup. Ask them to toss in some extra onions. The oil and onions will help to offset the higher glycemic value of the rice. Skip the steamed rice all together. The type of white rice served in most Asian restaurants has the highest glycemic level of all the rices. Any entree with broccoli or onions will help to control your blood sugar. Always skip the dishes with sweet sauces.

Steak House - Have fried cheese, mushrooms or onions as your appetizer, but be sure to share! A single person should never eat an entire onion blossom. Do order salad, but ask about the sugar content of the salad dressings. Bleu cheese and Caesar dressings are usually sugar-free. If in doubt, ask the waiter to bring vinegar and oil, then add it yourself. If available, order sweet potatoes with cinnamon and butter, but no sugar. Steamed vegetables are often available, as well. Absolutely do not order a baked white potato. Just think of the potato as a huge blob of sugar - that should help you resist the temptation. A small serving of onion rings can also be substituted for the baked potato.

Everyday Eating

Upon rising, 1 serving of fruit or fruit juice.

30 minutes later:
1 egg, prepared as desired
1 - 2 pieces whole grain toast
1 serving bacon or sausage, occasionally
coffee or tea, with real cream if desired (skip the creamers - they can raise the blood sugar)
or
Whole grain, sugar-free cereal (such as shredded wheat) with diluted half & half or cream
    (cream has far less milk-sugar than does milk)- sprinkle with fructose or alternative
    sweetener
coffee or tea (as above)

Mid-morning
Low glycemic snack, such as a handful of nuts or peanut butter spread on a whole grain cracker
(For other ideas, see *In a Hurry?* in the Table of Contents)

Lunch
Green leafy salad with sugar-free dressing, such as grilled chicken Caesar salad
or
Meat or protein based (like cheese or eggs) sandwich with whole grain bread
or
Peanut butter and sugar-free jelly on whole grain bread
or
Vegetable plate, with a small portion of meat as desired and whole grain roll

Mid-afternoon
Light, low glycemic snack

Dinner
Salad - leafy and green, with sugar-free dressing
1 serving meat
2 low-glycemic side dishes (or a double portion of 1 low-glycemic dish)
1 serving whole grain bread, if you have not eaten bread earlier in the day
1 serving dessert, such as cheese with wine, sugar-free jello, or sugar-free instant pudding.
Sugar-free ice cream is also nice, but try not to eat too many foods that contain artificial
sweeteners.

Evening snack
Small handful of nuts or low glycemic dessert, if you did not have it earlier, after dinner.

*One glass of red wine is allowed per day, only with food. If you reach a plateau or seem to lose
too slowly, then completely skip the wine. Listen to your body!

The Search for Low-Glycemic Foods

Your first stop can be in your local supermarket, but health food grocery stores have wonderful specialty items and more variety. The foods may seem more expensive, but you will not be wasting your money on junk food. You will be getting more nutrition for your dollar with whole foods than you ever did when you were spending money on empty calories. No longer will you suffer from eating binges. You will gradually find yourself satisfied with smaller portions, for your body will no longer be starved for real nutrition.

You can buy items such as fructose, agave syrup, dried fruits, and unsweetened coconut in bulk in the health food grocery stores. Fructose is especially expensive in those little boxes in the supermarket. Agave syrup is a more natural form of this sweetener. I could not find unsweetened coconut in any supermarket in my area, but did find it in dehydrated form in a health food grocery store. Better yet, buy a whole coconut and grate your own. I also found that the dried fruits that you buy in bulk in the health food grocery stores were tastier and larger than those that come pre-packaged. A few dried apricots are a very nice replacement for a candy bar.

When in the supermarket, be sure to look in the nutritional or dietary section. There, you can often find whole grain, sugar-free cereals and other useful products. There is even chocolate candy sweetened with fructose. The dark chocolate *Estee* bars are great for making cookies! *Lindt's 70% Excellence bar* is also a nice low-glycemic form of chocolate.

Do not substitute low-fat food for whole foods, such as sour cream, cheese, and salad dressings. The fat actually helps to keep your blood sugar at a better level by slowing the absorption of carbohydrates during digestion. Many products that are low fat and fat free have added sugars and starches to compensate for the loss of flavor and texture. As long as you keep your blood sugar at moderate levels, the fat is not going to cause you to gain weight.

Label reading will become an art form. You may be surprised to see how many products have sugar, molasses, corn, corn syrup (including high fructose corn syrup - not good), honey and wheat flour. Glucose, maltose, dextrose, and sucrose are all sugars that you should avoid. When you see any of these, it is best to look for an alternative product. The only exception to this can be found when you shop for whole grain yeast breads. Yeast needs some form of sugar in order to rise. The fiber in the whole grain breads will offset the small amount of sugar that is used to feed the yeast. If you choose to make your own bread, fructose works as well as table sugar (sucrose) and will eliminate the problem. Several delicious bread recipes are included in this book.

When it comes to food, natural packaging is the best. By this, I mean the packaging that nature itself gives to food. When we process grains and remove the outside of the package, nutrients and fiber are lost. The vitamins that manufacturers put back into the food do not truly bring the product back to its original nutritional value. Grains are in many products that we eat: cereals, breads, pastas, even sauces and gravies. They are essential to our health, but the whole grain provides optimal nutrition for you and your family.

Health food grocery stores have a wonderful variety of whole grain flours. Basic whole wheat (stone ground) flour is made from a hard wheat; whole grain pastry flour is ground from a softer variety. The harder the wheat, the lower the glycemic value. Kamut and spelt flours are more primitive forms of wheat and are often tolerated by individuals who are wheat sensitive. If you have that problem, give these more nutritious varieties a try. Of the three grains, kamut has the most delicate flavor. All are high in fiber and protein.

The number of whole grain, sugar-free cereals is limited, but growing. Health food grocery stores often have the best selection. *Kashi* is a nice mix of whole grains that you can have in moderate amounts. *Uncle Sam* cereal is also a good choice and has a whopping 10 grams of fiber per serving. Again, check the labels when you shop. Unless it says whole grain or stone ground, assume it is not.

More and more, whole grain breads are appearing on the supermarket shelf. But read the labels to be sure they are completely whole grain or stone ground - or as close as possible. The words wheat flour and whole meal do not mean whole grain. Try to choose the breads that have the sweetener listed as far near the end of the list of ingredients as possible. Ingredients are listed in the order of measure. Whatever is first is in the greatest amount. Just do the best you can to stay within the guidelines. You may have to compromise at times. When you find yourself in a place where your choices are limited, keep the servings smaller.

Be careful when buying whole grain pastas. Spelt pasta and whole wheat are your most healthful choices. However, the texture is not quite the same, and it may take a bit of time to adjust. Some of the smaller companies have pastas that are made of the hard wheat flours, such as durham and semolina and have a higher fiber content than the more popular brands. *Mendicino Pasta Co.* has a garlic basil pasta that has 6 grams of dietary fiber per serving and tastes delicious. *Eden* has pasta that is half whole grain and half durham flour, which is also acceptable. Check the brands in your area for their fiber content to see what is available. Do not buy pasta that contains less than 2 grams of fiber per serving and do cut the amount of pasta you normally eat in half. Be sure to serve protein with your pasta, as well.

Finding chips is another problem, since we are trying to avoid white potatoes and corn. Potato chips actually have a moderate glycemic value because of the high amount of fat they contain. However, there is almost no nutritive value in them, and the type of fat in which they are cooked can actually make them unhealthy. That leaves little to choose. *Terra Chips* and *Olive* Oil brand chips have salted sweet potato chips. *Kettle* brand has multi-grain tortilla chips with 2 grams per serving. Just be sure to check the label for the sugar and fiber content. Some of these products, unfortunately, do have sugar cane concentrate (another word for sugar). Avoid those. The amount of fiber in the chip is important. Fiber tends to lower the glycemic value of foods. When buying chips try to find those that have 2 or more grams of fiber per serving; then eat only a small amount. Measure how much you will eat, put it into a small bowl, and put the package away, out of sight.

The quest for crackers that are whole grain, without any form of sugar, was not easy. Again, there are very few in the supermarkets. The only mainstream cracker I have been able to find at this time is *Triscuits*. *Ryvita* is a brand of crisp bread that has several whole grain varieties, including one that is high in fiber. *Adrienne's Lavosh 10- Grain crackers* are very tasty and a nice choice to serve with cheese and dips. Check your nutritional section for specialty crackers. Again, health food grocery stores often have a better selection

Some very tasty jams available today are sugar-free. Unfortunately, many of them list as their first ingredient, grape juice concentrate. Grape sugar contains a large proportion of glucose. Fruit should be the first ingredient listed. Those sweetened with pear nectar, peach nectar, and apple juices are the best low glycemic choices. Just remember, jams are a condiment and should be eaten in small amounts. Some excellent butters (peach, pear and pumpkin) are also available at health food grocery stores. *Bionature*, sometimes carried in supermarkets, makes organic fruit spread sweetened with apple juice that you might enjoy.

Sugar-free peanut butter and mayonnaise are often available in the supermarket, but label reading is a must. *Duke's Mayonnaise* and *Smucker's Natural Peanut Butter* (the kind you have to stir) are two good choices that are widely available. Other brands may be available in other parts of the country. Almond butter is a healthy substitute for peanut butter.

Finding sugar-free salad dressings was another challenge. I was delighted to discover that bleu cheese and Caesar dressings are among the least likely to have added forms of sugar. Others are available, and the ingredients vary widely according to the brand. It seems that the smaller name brands are less likely to add sweeteners to their dressings than the major brands. Fat free dressings are the worst offenders because they often add sugar to compensate for flavor that is lost when the fat is removed. *Marie's Bleu Cheese* and some of *Cardini's* and *Jardine's Gourmet* dressings have some wonderful tasting dressings that are free of sugar. Read your labels. New dressings become available all the time.

Try to keep fresh fruit in your house, but avoid tropical fruits like pineapple and watermelon. Instead, choose temperate fruits like apples and pears and stone fruits like apricots and peaches. Organic is better, simply because organic produce has not been grown with chemicals and pesticides. They will not have chemical residue on their skins. It has been shown that organic fruits and vegetables are healthier for your body. However, their shelf life is shorter because they have not been sprayed with chemicals. The *Sugar Buster's* diet suggests eating fruit when you first rise in the morning. Then, wait 30 minutes to eat breakfast. Fresh fruit digests within 30 minutes, unlike other foods, which can take up to 2½ hours. If you have a condition that causes you to be insulin resistant, some nutritionists suggest that you eat a small piece of cheese with your fruit.

Be careful when buying meats. Many deli meats are cured with honey, sugar, or corn syrup. Instead, choose lean roast beef, turkey, Virginia-cured ham, corned beef and pastrami. If in doubt, ask the clerk to check the label for you.

If you are given the choice, buy meats that are organically raised. This is especially important if you have a problem related to excess male or female hormones, such as polycystic ovaries or Cushings syndrome. Menopausal women also should watch the amount of hormone-fed meat they consume. Commercially raised animals are fed hormones to produce larger animals. I have difficulty locating hormone-free meats in my area, but there are some places in the country where they are readily available. You may be lucky enough to live in one of those areas.

Organically raised chicken is called free-range chicken. The word *natural* does not mean free range. Eggs also are in this category, but are more easily available. If you can, choose eggs that come from chickens that have not been fed hormones and antibiotics. Nature's way is usually better, but we do not always have a choice.

When shopping for rice, choose raw brown rice. It has more fiber and nutrition than white, and nearly all white rice has a high glycemic value. Check the label. Some brown rices have more fiber than others. Be sure to read the labels and compare. The kind you have to rinse before cooking has the most fiber, and thus the lowest glycemic value. Some wonderful brown mixtures are available and are well worth the extra expense. *Lundberg* has several delicious brown rice mixes. These can sometimes be found with the rices and sometimes with the gourmet foods. You actually need smaller portions of the unprocessed rice because you feel more satisfied with less. Wild rice, which is not true rice, is also high in fiber and a tasty choice. Of the white rices, basmati has the lowest glycemic value, 58. Sticky rice is the worst, a whopping 98.

Healthier rices do take longer to cook. If this is a problem, just plan ahead. The preparation time is only a few minutes, but the cooking times are usually 50 to 60 minutes. You may want to cook the rice a day or so ahead of time. Refrigerate, and heat as needed. Or cook some up over the weekend and freeze. Rice reheats especially well in the microwave. The nutritional benefits are worth the effort for your family, and whole grain rice is not going to cause a surge in your blood sugar in the way as the higher glycemic white rice.

It will take several weeks for your body to adjust to food changes. It is possible that you will experience headaches and some light-headedness for the first two weeks. This just means that your body is looking for its sugar fix. After the adjustment period, you will find that your energy level is more constant. You should no longer crash several hours following a meal.

You can now enjoy butter (yes, butter, not margarine) on your whole grain toast, sauces on your meat and even an occasional fried dish. Cheese and red wine make a lovely dessert, even when eating out. Or finish your dinner with a cup of cappuccino topped with whipped cream and cinnamon. Giving up the sugar and excess starches is not so bad after you make the changes! Focus on all the wonderful foods that you can have, not on those you have chosen to give up.

To Sum It Up - Healthy Habits

1. **Fresh (uncooked) fruit is best eaten on an empty stomach** - 30 minutes before a meal or 2 hours after. This helps to prevent digestive and metabolic problems. Eaten with other foods, fruit may sit in your stomach and ferment, rather than move on through as it should.

2. **Avoid processed grains.** Instead, choose whole grain (stone-ground, not whole meal) breads, crackers, and pasta.

3. **Skip the white rice.** Brown and wild rices have more protein and fiber. Always reach for the whole grain versions.

4. **Never eat table sugar.** Honey, molasses, and corn syrup are also high glycemic forms of sugar and will raise your insulin just as badly.

5. **White potatoes and corn have to go.** Both raise your blood sugar so much that they are mostly stored as fat. You may as well open the sugar bowl and dig in!

6. **Fat is not your enemy.** As long as your insulin is at low to moderate levels, a moderate amount of fat is fine. In fact, the human body needs a certain amount of fat. Some fats are even essential to your health.

7. **Nuts are a great snack**, especially almonds, macadamia nuts, and pecans, packed with essential fatty acids. Have a handful in the afternoon or late night. A small handful is both healthful and satisfying as one of your snacks.

8. **Salads and leafy green vegetables are essential.** Just be sure there is no sugar in the dressings. A little butter or olive oil is fine for flavor. Leafy lettuces, such as romaine, are high in folic acid - very heart healthy.

9. **Eat lots of green and yellow vegetables.** They are packed with fiber and nutrition. Sweet potatoes in moderation are an especially nice substitute for white potatoes or corn.

10. **Be sure to eat a small amount of low glycemic carbohydrates when you eat protein.** Proteins eaten alone can raise your blood sugar.

11. **Caffeine should be avoided**, but if you absolutely must have it, be sure to consume your caffeine with a bite of food. This helps to keep the blood sugar from surging.

12. **Other things** that can cause your blood sugar to spike: nicotine, estrogen, and certain medications.

13. **Do eat carbohydrates after intensive exercise**, but try to stay with those that have a lower glycemic value. Carbohydrates help repair muscle and replace glucose that has been pulled from your muscles.

14. **Be reasonable in the sizes of your food portions.** One serving is usually equal to 1/2 cup. It is just fine to have a second serving, but be sure that you are eating vegetables with your meat and whole grain bread! Eating lower glycemic foods does not give you permission to eat unlimited amounts of food. In fact, after you have eliminated high glycemic foods from your diet, your food cravings will decrease.

15. **Cold pressed oils are the healthiest.** Choose extra virgin olive oil, over the other olive oils. It is the unrefined oils that have the healthful nutrients and is well worth the extra expense. Healthy oils are cold-pressed, not heated or processed.

16. **Eating three moderate meals a day and several small snacks** (always avoiding high glycemic foods) is the way to success. Don't skip meals. Protein, carbohydrates, and fats should all be included in your diet.

17. **Drink lots of water**. Try to drink a minimum of 8 glasses each day. Coffee, tea and other such drinks should not be counted as part of your water intake.

18. **Sweetened foods should be an occasional treat.** A steady diet of sweetened foods, even those artificially sweetened, prevents you from getting the nutrition you need.

19. **If you yield to occasional temptation,** as we all do, don't get upset with yourself. Just start fresh at the next meal. Do not give up. It is well worth changing to healthy eating habits. You will never be sorry!

Recipes

Nutritional information is included for those who are following diets that require nutritional counts or for those who need the food exchanges for each recipe. Most low-glycemic diets do not depend on these counts. Just remember that not all carbohydrates are created equal. These recipes use carbs that have been found to be lower glycemic in nature and should not send your insulin surging out of control.

Splenda in the recipes refers to the pourable, granular form (that measures like sugar) unless otherwise noted. Your favorite alternative granular sweetener like maltitol and acesulfame potassium (K) may be substituted for Splenda.

Appetizers & Snacks

Classic Guacamole
Ole!

2 ripe avocados, peeled and pitted
1 tablespoon finely grated onion
1 tablespoon lemon or lime juice
1 teaspoon salt
¼ teaspoon chili powder
1 tablespoon sugar free mayonnaise

Peel and pit the avocado. The easiest way is to slice the avocado in half, lengthwise, then run your finger under the peel to separate it from the fruit. Carefully, pop a sharp knife into the center of the seed and twist to remove the seed. It will come out easily if the avocado is ripe.

Mash the avocados with a fork. Stir in the remaining ingredients. Cover with plastic wrap, pressing the wrap to the dip until ready to serve. This helps to keep the dip from darkening. Refrigerate. Serve with black bean cakes or Tex-Mex dishes. Even better, use guacamole as your bread spread on whole grain sandwiches.

Serves 8.

1 serving: Total Fat (g): 9
                Protein (g): 1
                Total Carbohydrates (g): 4
                Dietary Fiber (g): 1
                94 calories

Food Exchanges: Fat: 1½

Chunky Guacamole

1 ripe tomato
2 ripe avocadoes
2 tablespoons mayonnaise
juice of 1 lime (2 to 3 tablespoons) 2 tablespoons diced red onion
½ teaspoon salt
¼ teaspoon chili powder
1 tablespoon freshly chopped cilantro

It is not necessary, but if desired, peel the tomato. It is easiest to first place the tomato in very hot water for about 30 seconds; then the peel should slip off easily. Cut the tomato in half and remove the seeds and pulp with your fingers. Discard the seeds and pulp. Dice the meat of the tomato and set aside.

Peel and pit the avocado. The easiest way is to slice the avocado in half, lengthwise, then run your finger under the peel to separate it from the fruit. Carefully, pop a sharp knife into the center of the seed and twist to remove the seed. It will come out easily if the avocado is ripe.

Slice; then mash the avocado with the mayonnaise and the lime juice. Leave the mixture a little chunky. Add the tomatoes, onion, salt, chili powder and cilantro. Stir with a fork, but do not mash.

Place in a non-metal container and top with plastic wrap, pressing the wrap into the surface of the dip until ready to serve to prevent the surface from turning brown.

Serves 8.

1 serving: Total Fat (g): 11
               Protein (g): 1
               Total Carbohydrates (g): 5
               Dietary Fiber (g): 1
               99 calories

Exchanges: Fat: 2

Serve with sliced jicama instead of chips, as an accompaniment to Tex-Mex dishes or as a sandwich spread.

Black Bean Cakes
Quick and easy!

2 (15 ounce) cans black beans, rinsed and drained
2 eggs, beaten
1 small onion, minced
1 clove garlic, crushed
½ teaspoon salt
¼ teaspoon ground cumin
dash Tabasco
2 tablespoons whole wheat flour*
¼ cup + 1 tablespoon canola oil, divided

In a small pan, sauté the onion until translucent. Add garlic and continue to sauté for 1 minute. Set aside.

In a medium bowl, lightly mash beans until broken, but not pasty. Add all other ingredients, including the onions and mix gently.

In a large skillet, preheat ¼ inch of oil in pan on medium-high (until a drop of water sizzles when added). Drop the bean mixture by large spoonfuls into hot oil; flatten gently with second spoon or spatula.

Cook about 5 minutes per side, turning once. Cakes should be lightly browned. Drain on paper towels.

Serve with sour cream and salsa. May be used as a side dish or an appetizer.

Makes 6 (4 inch) cakes.

Per cake: Total Fat (g): 14 (includes oil from frying)
　　　　　Protein (g): 10
　　　　　Total Carbohydrates (g): 22
　　　　　Dietary Fiber (g): 8
　　　　　Calories: 259

Food Exchanges: Starch/Bread: 1½ Lean Meat: 1, Vegetable: ½, Fat: 2½

Spelt or kamut flour may be substituted.

Olive Tartlets

A wonderful little appetizer, filled with the goodness of whole grains and olives.

Parmesan Cheese Pastry

¼ cup whole-wheat flour
½ cup Parmesan cheese
2 tablespoons oat bran
1/8 teaspoon salt
2 tablespoons softened butter
1 tablespoon water

Filling

4 ounces cream cheese
½ cup sliced green pimento-stuffed olives, drained
1 egg
1/8 teaspoon cayenne pepper, or to taste

Preheat oven to 350 degrees. Grease a miniature muffin tin (sized for 12 muffins) and set aside.

In a small bowl, mix the flour, cheese, oat bran and salt. Work the butter into the dry ingredients with a pastry blender or a fork, until blended. Add 1 tablespoon water and mix with a fork until evenly moistened. Divide the dough among the 12 tins and press the dough into each, lining the bottoms and sides. Set aside.

Place all the filling ingredients in a food processor and blend. Divide the filling into the 12 cups. Top each with an olive slice and piece of pimento. Place in the oven and bake 20 minutes. Cool 10 minutes; then remove to a serving platter. Serve warm.

Makes 12 miniature tartlets.

1 tartlet: Total Fat (g): 7
           Protein (g): 3
           Total Carbohydrates (g): 3
           Dietary Fiber (g): 1
           88 calories

Exchanges: Lean Meat: ½; Fat: 1

Caramelized Onion Tart with Rosemary Crust

Filling

5 slices sugar-free bacon
1 tablespoon butter
4 large sweet onions, sliced (about 10 cups)

In a large skillet, cook bacon until crisp. Remove to cool. Crumble.

Add butter and onion and cook over medium high heat, stirring, until the onion begins to brown. Reduce heat and add bacon crumbles. Simmer and cook, uncovered, until the onion is the consistency of jam, about 1 hour. Stir as needed. May be made a day ahead and refrigerated. If so, increase baking time by 5 minutes.

Rosemary Crust

1 cup whole grain pastry flour
½ cup oat bran
½ teaspoon salt
½ teaspoon dried rosemary
½ cup grated Parmesan cheese
½ cup butter, melted
2 tablespoons cold water

Preheat the oven to 450 degrees.

In large bowl, mix flour, oat bran, salt, rosemary, and cheese. Stir in the butter with a fork until the mixture is crumbly and evenly mixed. Sprinkle cold water over the mixture and stir with a fork until mixed.

Place the mixture in a tart pan and press evenly along the sides and bottom. Fill with onion mixture and place in the preheated oven. Reduce heat to 350 degrees. Bake 30 to 35 minutes, until edges of crusts are browned. Remove from the oven. Serve warm or at room temperature.

Makes about 10 appetizer servings.

Per Serving: Total Fat (g): 13
Protein (g): 7
Total Carbohydrates (g): 22
Dietary Fiber (g): 4
Calories: 224

Food Exchanges: Starch/Bread: 1, Lean Meat: ½, Vegetable: 1½, Fat: 2½

Chicago Style Pizza with Parmesan Basil Crust
Yes, you can have pizza. Just add your favorite toppings!

Chicago Pizza Crust:
1 cup whole wheat pastry flour*
½ cup oat bran
½ teaspoon salt
1½ tablespoons dried basil
½ cup grated Parmesan cheese
½ cup extra virgin olive oil
2 tablespoons cold water

1 can sugar-free pizza sauce (*Muir* is a good one)
8 ounces shredded mozzarella
Additional toppings, as desired.

Preheat the oven to 450 degrees. Grease a square 10-inch baking dish or brownie pan.

Mix flour, oat bran, salt, basil, and Parmesan cheese. Mix in the olive oil with a fork. Sprinkle 2 tablespoon cold water over mixture, then quickly combine with a fork, until the dough holds together. Press into a 10-inch square pan on bottom and slightly up the sides. Bake 10 minutes.

Remove from the oven and top with pizza sauce, then mozzarella cheese. If desired, add additional topping (see below). Return to oven.

Reduce heat to 375 degrees. Bake 15 to 20 minutes, until the cheese is melted and <u>just begins</u> to brown.

Serves 4 to 6.

1/6 of pizza: Total Fat (g): 32
Protein (g): 16
Total Carbohydrates (g): 25
Dietary Fiber (g): 4
425 calories

Food Exchanges: Starch/Bread: 1½ Lean Meat: 1½, Vegetable: 1, Fat: 5½

Suggested low-glycemic toppings:
cooked ground beef or sausage; vegetables, such as onions, peppers, mushrooms, spinach, broccoli or sliced olives; feta cheese. Be creative and enjoy!

Snackin' Nuts
A handful in the afternoon or at bedtime makes a great snack.

1 cup whole almonds
1 cup whole pecans
1 cup unsalted roasted peanuts
1 cup walnuts

For each variation, spread the nuts on a jellyroll pan or cookie sheet and bake at 300 degrees for 10 minutes. A jellyroll pan works best because it has sides to keep the nuts from spilling.

While the nuts are in the oven, prepare the flavoring as below; then continue as directed.

1/4 cup: Total Fat (g): 18
                Protein (g): 7
                Total Carbohydrates (g): 6
                Dietary Fiber (g): 3
                196 calories

Food Exchanges: Starch/Bread: ½, Lean Meat: 1, Fat: 3

Hot 'n Spicy Nuts

¼ cup butter
1 tablespoon hot sauce
1 tablespoon soy sauce
1½ teaspoons salt
1 teaspoon dried mustard
dash cayenne pepper, to taste

Heat butter until just melted. Stir in the remaining ingredients. After removing the nuts from the oven, pour the nuts into a large bowl. Pour the butter mixture over and stir well. Spread the nuts on a jellyroll pan once more and bake 20 additional minutes, stirring once. Remove and spread on paper towels to cool. Stir in an airtight container.

1/4 cup: Total Fat (g): 21
                Protein (g): 7
                Total Carbohydrates (g): 6
                Dietary Fiber (g): 3
                223 calories

Food Exchanges: Starch/Bread: ½, Lean Meat: 1, Fat: 3

Sweetly Spiced Nuts

¼ cup butter
1½ teaspoons ground cinnamon
¼ teaspoon ground cardamom
1½ tablespoons fructose or alternative sweetener

Heat butter until just melted. Stir in cinnamon and cardamom. After removing nuts from oven, pour nuts into large bowl. Pour the butter mixture over and stir well. Spread nuts on jelly roll once more and bake 20 additional minutes, stirring once. Remove and spread on paper towels. Sprinkle with fructose and cool. Store in airtight container

Each recipe makes 4 cups.

1/4 cup: Total Fat (g): 21
                   Protein (g): 7
                   Total Carbohydrates (g): 6(using fructose)
                   Dietary Fiber (g): 3
                   225 calories

Food Exchanges: Starch/Bread: ½, Lean Meat: 1, Fat: 3

Onion Stuffed Baby Bellas

Chromium rich mushrooms filled with cheese and onions. What a terrific and tasty combination for controlling insulin surges! Make this recipe ahead of time, and then pop it in the oven just before your friends arrive.

10 ounces baby bella mushrooms (about 16)
1 cup diced sweet onions
2 teaspoons butter
1 tablespoon oat bran
1 cup finely shredded Swiss cheese
1/8 teaspoon mace

Spray an 8-inch square baking dish with oil. Preheat the oven to 350 degrees.

Gently rinse the mushrooms and dry with a paper towel. Remove and discard the stems; lay the caps upside-down in baking dish.

Melt the butter in a small skillet. Add the onions and sauté until translucent and just beginning to brown. Remove from heat; then, stir in the oat bran, cheese, and mace. Combine.

Fill each mushroom cap with the onion mixture, gently pressing mixture into the cap and dividing the mixture evenly among the mushrooms.

Bake 12 minutes. Then, turn on the broiler and broil the mushrooms for 2 to 3 minutes, until the tops are bubbly. Serve warm.

Makes 16 stuffed mushrooms.

1 stuffed mushroom: Total Fat (g): 2
Protein (g): 3
Total Carbohydrates (g): 2
Dietary Fiber (g): 3

Food Exchanges: Lean Meat: ½, Fat: ½, Vegetable: ½

Pecan Stuffed Mushrooms
Perfectly scrumptious; prepare ahead of time and cook when ready!

16 large fresh mushrooms
2 teaspoons butter
¼ cup onion, finely minced
1 (3 ounce) package cream cheese, softened
2 tablespoons oat bran
¼ cup grated Parmesan cheese
¼ cup finely chopped pecans

Wash and dry the mushrooms. Remove stems and discard.

Sauté the onion in butter until translucent. Remove to a medium bowl and mix in the remaining ingredients.

Fill each mushroom cap with about 1 tablespoon pecan mixture. Bake at 350 degrees for about 10 minutes or until hot.

Turn on the broiler until the tops bubble and begin to brown. Remove to a pretty platter and serve.

Makes 16 appetizers.

Per appetizer: Total Fat (g): 4
Protein (g): 2
Total Carbohydrates (g): 2
Dietary Fiber (g): trace
48 calories

Food Exchanges: Fat: ½

Grilled Portobello Mushrooms
Nice as an appetizer or as a sandwich between slices of whole-grain bread.

12 ounces thickly sliced portobello mushrooms
2 tablespoons olive oil
1 clove garlic, crushed
¼ teaspoon salt
pepper to taste

Heat the grill. Combine all ingredients except the mushrooms. Brush the mushrooms with the oil mixture. Place on a hot grill, turning after 5 minutes or until the heated side is crisp.

Alternative cooking method:
Heat a non-stick skillet on medium-high. Add mushrooms that have been brushed with oil and braise until crispy on both sides.

Serve as a side dish or an appetizer.

Serves 3 to 6.

1/6 recipe: Total Fat (g): 5
                 Protein (g): 1
                 Total Carbohydrates (g): 3
                 Dietary Fiber (g): 1
                 54 calories

Food Exchanges: Vegetable: 3, Fat: 1

Portobello Mushroom Sandwich:
On toasted whole-grain bread, spread 1-tablespoon herbed cheese spread. Top with a grilled Portobello mushroom slice, Swiss cheese, and crumbled, cooked bacon. Briefly place under broiler and heat until the cheese is melted.

Cheese Straws
Party time!

1 cup butter, softened
2 cups shredded, extra sharp cheese, room temperature
1¾ cups whole wheat or spelt flour (fluff with spoon before measuring)
½ teaspoon salt
½ teaspoon ground cayenne pepper
1 teaspoon lemon juice

Preheat the oven to 300 degrees.

Using a mixer, beat the butter at medium speed until creamy. Gradually add the cheese, beating well. Add flour, salt, and pepper. Beat at low speed until blended. Add lemon juice and beat for 15 minutes at medium speed.

Pipe the mixture from a pastry bag or drop dough by teaspoonfuls onto ungreased baking sheets.

Bake for about 12 minutes, until set. Cool on wire racks.

Yield: 6 dozen

4 straws: Total Fat (g): 15
          Protein (g): 5
          Total Carbohydrates (g): 9
          Dietary Fiber (g): 1
          181 calories

Food Exchanges: Starch/Bread: ½, Lean Meat: ½, Fat: 2½

Fruit & Nut Tabouli

1¼ cups boiling water
½ cup bulgur (specialty grains and health food sections of your grocery)
2 tablespoons lemon juice
½ cup dried cranberries
1 apple, peeled, cored and finely chopped (about 1 cup)
2 tablespoons olive oil
¼ cup minced onion
¼ cup finely chopped walnuts
½ cucumber, peeled, seeded and finely chopped
¼ cup finely chopped celery with tops
1 teaspoon grated fresh ginger
¼ teaspoon salt

Measure the bulgur into a bowl; pour the boiling water over and cover with a plate for 20 minutes.

While waiting, put the lemon juice into a large bowl and add the cranberries. Peel, core and chop the apple. Add to the lemon juice and toss together. Add all remaining ingredients, except the bulgur.

After the 20 minutes of steeping, drain the bulgur in a finely meshed strainer, gently pressing out the excess moisture. Add to the bowl of ingredients and serve.

This dish is nice served freshly warm, at room temperature, or cold the next day! Refrigerate unused portions.

Makes 8 (½ cup) servings.

1 serving: Total Fat (g): 6
                Protein (g): 2
                Total Carbohydrates (g): 11
                Dietary Fiber (g): 3
                100 calories

Food Exchanges: Starch/Bread: ½, Fat: 1

This can be used as a salad or a dip. If used as a dip, serve with jicama or cucumber slices!

Summer Peach Salsa

Relax with this light summer salsa! Served with jicama slices for dipping, this appetizer is loaded with fiber, potassium and calcium.

1 jicama, peeled and sliced
juice of 1 lime
1-2 ripe peaches, diced (about 1 cup)
½ cup fresh blueberries
½ sweet onion, minced
¼ teaspoon freshly grated ginger

Pour the lime juice into a medium bowl. Peel and dice the peaches and add to the bowl, tossing to coat the peaches. Add the remaining ingredients and combine all. Place in a pretty bowl and serve with jicama slices for "dipping".

Serves 6 to 8.

1/6 recipe without jicama: Total Fat (g): 0
Protein (g): 0
Total Carbohydrates (g): 7
Dietary Fiber (g): 1
33calories

Food Exchanges: Fruit: ½

½ cup sliced jicama: Total Fat (g): 21
Protein (g): 0
Total Carbohydrates (g): 9
Dietary Fiber (g): 5
41 calories

Food Exchanges: Starch/Bread: ½

Peach Party Pate

Light, creamy, and easy to whip up, this unusual pate is delightful for a friendly gathering or an elegant evening. Serve with whole grain crackers to keep the glycemic level of the dish low.

16 ounces cream cheese
4 large eggs
½ cup heavy
½ cup + 2 tablespoons sour cream, divided
2 large, ripe peaches, peeled and cut into pieces
1/8 teaspoon almond extract
½ teaspoon vanilla extract
1 additional peach for garnish (optional)
Fruit-fresh or lime juice

Butter or spray a 10-inch glass or ceramic quiche dish or pie pan. If using a spray, be sure to use one that is butter-flavored or neutral in flavor. Preheat oven to 325 degrees.

Combine all ingredients except 2 tablespoons sour cream and the one peach for garnishing and process in a blender or food processor. Pour into greased dish and place in preheated oven.

Bake about 40 minutes, until a knife inserted in center comes out clean. Remove and cool. Evenly spread the reserved 2 tablespoons of sour cream over the top. Refrigerate.

Before serving, peel and cut the additional peach into thin slices. Lightly toss with Fruit Fresh (ascorbic acid) or a small amount of lime juice to preserve the color. Arrange slices on top of the pate.

To serve, place the dish of pate on the center of a round tray. Surround with a selection of whole grain crackers and enjoy.

Serves 12.

1 serving: Total Fat (g): 20
                Protein (g): 5
                Total Carbohydrates (g): 4
                Dietary Fiber (g): tr
                216 calories

Food Exchanges: Lean Meat: ½, Fat: 3½

Stuffed Apricots

5 dozen dried apricots (about 1¼ cups)

Filling:
8 ounces cream cheese
½ cup silken tofu
1 teaspoon cinnamon
½ teaspoon ground ginger
½ teaspoon ground nutmeg
1 tablespoon Whey Low (fructose, agave nectar or Splenda may be used)

¼ cup finely chopped walnuts

Using a narrow knife, such as a paring knife, make a slit on the end of each apricot, twisting the knife to open the inside. Set aside.

Mix cream cheese, tofu, spices and sweetener together. Place the mixture in a pastry bag, using a wider tip. Pipe the cream cheese mixture into each apricot. Dip the cream cheese end of each apricot into the finely chopped nuts. Arrange on tray; refrigerate until ready to serve.

Makes about 5 dozen stuffed apricots.

4 appetizers: Total Fat (g): 7
Protein (g): 2
Total Carbohydrates (g): 8
Dietary Fiber (g): 1
50 calories

Food Exchanges: Fruit: ½

Cinnamon Cream Cheese Triangles

8 ounces cream cheese, softened
¼ cup soft silken tofu
1 teaspoon cinnamon
1 tablespoon Splenda or granular alternative sweetener
2/3 cup finely chopped pecans
32 slices thin sliced whole wheat bread

In a small bowl, combine the first five ingredients.

Cut crusts from bread, if desired. Spread half the bread slices with the cream cheese mixture; top each with second bread slice. Cut each diagonally twice, making an "X". This will make 4 appetizer triangles from each sandwich.

Makes 64 appetizer triangles.

1 tablespoon spread (2 triangles):   Total Fat (g): 4
Protein (g): 1
Total Carbohydrates (g): 1
Dietary Fiber (g): tr
41 calories

Food Exchanges: (spread for 2 triangles): Fat: 1½

*Because brands can vary, bread counts are not given; check your bread package and add to your totals.

In a Hurry? Low Glycemic Quick Bites

Cinnamon Toast:
Spread a *slice of whole grain bread* with *softened butter*. Sprinkle with *cinnamon-fructose*. Place underneath broiler and broil until topping is bubbly, about 1 - 2 minutes. Be careful not to burn.

Cinnamon-Fructose Mixture:
Mix *2/3-cup fructose* with *1-tablespoon cinnamon*. Store in an airtight container.

Cheese Toast:
Sprinkle *slice of whole grain bread* with *cheddar cheese*. Place underneath broiler and broil until cheese is melted and begins to brown, just a few minutes. Top with a bit of *sugar-free jam*, if desired.

French Toast:
Melt - *tablespoon butter* in skillet. Beat *one egg* with *1-teaspoon water*. Dip both sides of *whole grain bread slices* in egg mixture. Fry in skillet over medium heat, turning when browned. (1) Remove and sprinkle with *cinnamon-fructose*. (2) Or, omit the cinnamon-fructose and top with a slice of *Swiss cheese* and *thinly sliced ham* that has been browned in the same skillet.

Quesadillas:
Spray skillet with non-stick spray and place over medium heat. Lay one *whole-wheat or low-carb tortilla* on a skillet. Sprinkle about *¼-cup shredded Colby-jack or cheddar cheese* on tortilla. Top with *additional tortilla*. When cheese melts and the top tortilla sticks to cheese, turn the tortilla over and heat for an additional minute or two, until lightly browned. Remove to a plate and slice into wedges. Serve with *salsa and sour cream*.

Sweet Potatoes:
Bake ahead (one hour in oven at 400 degrees) and store in refrigerator, up to a week. To eat, cut off one end, wrap bottom half of potato with waxed paper and push potato up from bottom. This is great for breakfast on the run. If the sweet potato is large, cut in half for two portions.

Rabbit Roll-ups:
On a *large leaf of lettuce or spinach*, spread toppings as listed below. After covering lettuce leaf with topping, roll up from one end and eat as finger food. Have fun making your own variations.

1. Spread with *sugar-free mayonnaise*. Top with *shredded cheese* and *thinly sliced luncheon meat*.

2. Spread with *sour cream*. Sprinkle with *shredded cheese* and *salsa*.

3. Sprinkle with *shredded spinach*. Top with crumbled *feta cheese* and drizzle with *sugar free Italian dressing*.

4. Spread with *sugar-free mayonnaise*. Top with *salami and ham*, thinly sliced. Add

thinly sliced tomato, shredded lettuce, and *diced hot peppers*. Sprinkle with *basil*, a pinch of *oregano*, *vinegar* and *oil.*

Triscuits:

Top with any low-glycemic topping. Try topping a small plateful of *Triscuits* with your favorite shredded cheese. Microwave until melted and bubbly. Use the new thin *Triscuits* with dips.

Celery Sticks:

Wash. Cut into 3-inch lengths and fill with *peanut butter* or *sugar-free cheese spread.*

Chocolate Drops:

Melt *2 Estee Dark Chocolate Bars* or *Lindt 70% Cocoa bars* . Quickly stir in *1-cup almonds*. Drop by teaspoonfuls onto *waxed paper*. Cool and store in airtight container.

Ryvita:

Spread 1 *Ryvita (preferably with added fiber) or other whole grain crisp-bread* with *sugar-free peanut butter* and <u>small amount</u> of *sugar-free jam.*

Eggs:

Boiled, scrambled or in an omelet, *eggs* are a quick, high protein food that will stay with you. My favorite is a southwestern omelet. It is a good idea to have a piece of *whole grain toast or a whole grain cracker* to balance out the protein and help your metabolism work more efficiently.

Egg Dishes

Dilled Deviled Eggs
For a picnic in the park!

1 dozen large eggs
¼ cup sugar-free mayonnaise
2 tablespoons white wine vinegar
1 teaspoon dry mustard
¼ teaspoon salt
dash black pepper
¼ teaspoon dried dill
paprika

Cover the eggs with cold water in a medium saucepan. Bring to a boil; reduce heat to medium, so that the water remains at a low boil. Boil for 15 minutes. Immediately drain water and place eggs in cold water. Crack the shells and peel. If you do not do this immediately, the eggs will be difficult to peel.

Slice the eggs in half lengthwise; remove the yolks to a medium bowl. Arrange the whites on a platter. To the yolks, add mayonnaise, mustard, salt, pepper, dill weed and vinegar. Mix with a fork until smooth and creamy. With a teaspoon, fill the whites with the yolk mixture. Lightly sprinkle with paprika. Refrigerate until ready to serve.

Serves 8 to 12.

2 halves: Total Fat (g): 8
               Protein (g): 6
               Total Carbohydrates (g): 1
               Dietary Fiber (g): trace
               99 calories

Food Exchanges: Lean Meat: 1, Fat: 1

Southwestern Omelet

3 tablespoons olive oil, divided
1 small onion, chopped
1 medium jalapeno pepper, seeded and finely minced
1 medium tomato, seeded and diced
4 eggs
1 cup Colby jack cheese, shredded

Heat 2 tablespoons of the oil in a small skillet over medium-high. Add the onion and pepper. Sauté until the onion is translucent. Gently add tomatoes and remove from heat. (Be sure all seeds and pulp are removed from the tomato before dicing.)

In a medium skillet, heat 1-tablespoon olive oil. Quickly whisk ¼-cup water into the eggs, mixing well. Pour the egg mixture into the skillet. Reduce heat to low. Cook about 5 minutes, gently lifting the edges to allow the egg mixture to run underneath to speed cooking.

When the top of the mixture is set, spread the onion mixture over half of the omelets. Top with cheese. With a spatula, lift the bare half of omelets and fold over the top of the cheese. Remove from skillet and serve.

Serves 2.

½ recipe: Total Fat (g): 47
          Protein (g): 26
          Total Carbohydrates (g): 11
          Dietary Fiber (g): 2
          563 calories

Food Exchanges: Lean Meat: 3 ½, Vegetable: 1 ½, Fat: 7 ½

Zucchini & Onion Frittata

½ cup Swiss cheese
3 slices whole grain bread, processed into crumbs, divided
4 eggs
1 cup sour cream
¼ cup olive oil
3 cups zucchini (about 3 medium), sliced into ¼ inch slices
1½ cups thinly sliced onion

Preheat the oven to 350 degrees. Heavily oil a soufflé or casserole dish; set aside. Reserve ½ cup breadcrumbs, setting; set aside.

Combine cheese with the remaining breadcrumbs; set aside.

With a fork or whisk, thoroughly mix the eggs with the sour cream and reserved breadcrumbs; set aside.

In large skillet, heat the olive oil on medium-high heat. Sear the zucchini about 2 minutes per side. Remove to the casserole and evenly distribute. Pour half egg mixture over.

Drain excess oil from the skillet. Return to heat. Add onions and cook until the onions just begin to brown. Layer them over zucchini. Pour remaining egg mixture evenly over. Press down.

Top with cheese and bread mixture. Bake 40 minutes, or until set and top is browned.

Serves 4 - 5.

1/4 recipe: Total Fat (g): 35
           Protein (g): 16
           Total Carbohydrates (g): 24
           Dietary Fiber (g): 4
           468 calories

Food Exchanges: Starch/Bread: 1, Lean Meat: 1½, Vegetable: 1, Fat: 6

Broccoli Frittata

3 eggs, beaten
2 cups sour cream
2 slices whole grain bread, processed into crumbs
½ cup Parmesan cheese
¼ teaspoon nutmeg
2 tablespoons olive oil
2/3 cup chopped onion
3 (10 ounces) packages chopped broccoli

Preheat oven to 350 degrees. Heavily oil 9x13 inch casserole.

Thoroughly mix the eggs, sour cream, cheese, nutmeg and bread crumbs with a fork or wire whisk. Set aside.

Heat the oil in a medium skillet. Add the onions and cook until translucent. Meanwhile, microwave the broccoli 2 - 3 minutes, until thawed. Add the broccoli to the onions and continue cooking until excess moisture is gone. Remove from heat. Pour into the prepared casserole. Pour the egg mixture over broccoli and onions.

Bake for 50 minutes, or until the frittata is puffy and set in the center.

Serves 6 - 8.

1/6 recipe: Total Fat (g): 25
Protein (g): 14
Total Carbohydrates (g): 19
Dietary Fiber (g): 6
349 calories

Food Exchanges: Starch/Bread: ½, Lean Meat: 1, Vegetable: 1, Fat: 4½

Three Alarm Frittata
Some like it hot!

Non-stick spray
1 (7 ounce) can chipotle peppers in adobe sauce
2 cups shredded cheddar
8 eggs
2 cups heavy cream
2 avocados
juice of one lime
1 jar salsa (optional)

Preheat the oven to 350 degrees.

Drain the peppers and reserve the sauce. Thinly slice the peppers and place them over the bottom of a 3-quart casserole. Sprinkle cheddar over the peppers.

Beat the eggs and cream together. Pour over the cheese and peppers.

Bake about 45 minutes or until the center is puffy. A knife inserted in the center will have a slight amount of cheese, but will be fairly clean. Remove from the oven and let stand 5 - 10 minutes.

While the frittata is baking, peel and slice the avocados into wedges and toss the in the lime juice to coat the avocado. Arrange on a small plate to serve on the side. The avocado has a nice cooling effect. Salsa adds a festive touch.

Serves 8.

1 serving: Total Fat (g): 43
               Protein (g): 16
               Total Carbohydrates (g): 7
               Dietary Fiber (g): 2
               467 calories

Food Exchanges: Lean Meat: 2, Vegetable: ½, Fat: 7½

Chile Rellenos Frittata
Perfect for Brunch

Non-stick spray
2 (4 ounce) cans diced green chiles
2 cups Colby cheese
8 eggs
2 cups heavy cream
1 jar salsa (optional)

Preheat oven to 350 degrees.

Spray a 3-quart casserole with non-stick spray.

Sprinkle chiles across the bottom of the casserole. Top with cheese.

Using a fork, beat the eggs with the cream. Pour over the cheese and chiles.

Bake about 45 minutes. The center will become puffy when done. A knife in center will be fairly clean, but may have cheese on it. Remove and let stand 5 - 10 minutes.

Serves 8.

If desired, serve with salsa.

1/8 recipe: Total Fat (g): 36
Protein (g): 13
Total Carbohydrates (g): 5
Dietary Fiber (g): 0
392 calories

Food Exchanges: Lean Meat: 1½, Vegetable: ½, Fat: 6

Classic Quiche Lorraine
Serve with a salad for a super supper!

Swiss Cheese Pastry
1 cup whole-wheat flour
½ cup oat bran
½ teaspoon salt
½ cup butter, softened
2 cups grated Swiss cheese, room temperature

Filling
8 strips bacon, cooked, drained and crumbled (reserve the fat)
½ cup onion, thinly sliced
1 cup Swiss cheese
¼ cup Parmesan cheese
4 eggs, lightly beaten
2 cups heavy cream
¼ teaspoon nutmeg
½ teaspoon salt
¼ teaspoon white pepper

Preheat the oven to 450 degrees.

To make the pastry, mix the dry ingredients in a medium bowl. Add the butter and cheese; mix thoroughly. Make the pastry into a ball. Roll between two sheets of waxed paper until it is about 2 inches larger in diameter than quiche pan a (9-inch pie pan may be used). To do this, wet the counter top with a damp cloth. Place one sheet of waxed paper on a damp counter so that it will stick. Place the pastry on this, and then top with the other piece of paper. Remove one side of paper and place the pastry, dough-side-down on the quiche pan. Remove the remaining paper and press the dough into place. Trim the edges evenly. Bake the crust 5 minutes. Remove from the oven.

To make the quiche filling, sauté the onion in the reserved bacon fat. Remove to paper towels, and then place the onion across bottom of pan. Add bacon and cheeses, placing them evenly across bottom of pan.

Combine the remaining ingredients and pour over the cheese, bacon and onions.

Bake 15 minutes. Reduce the oven heat to 350 degrees. Bake until a knife inserted at least one inch from center is clean, about 30 additional minutes. Let stand 10 minutes before slicing.

Serves 8.

1 serving: Total Fat (g): 28
Protein (g): 22
Total Carbohydrates (g): 19
Dietary Fiber (g): 3
616 calories

Food Exchanges: Starch/Bread: 1, Lean Meat: 2½, Fat: 9

Bread

Whole Wheat Cheddar Bread
Crusty and light textured - Perfect for sandwiches!

2 teaspoons dry yeast
1 cup + 2 tablespoons warm water (110 degrees), divided
¼ teaspoons + 1 tablespoon fructose, divided
1 teaspoon salt
3 cups whole-wheat flour (fluff with spoon before measuring)
1 cup sharp cheddar cheese, grated, room temperature

Add the yeast and ¼ teaspoon fructose to ¼ cup warm water. Let stand ten minutes or until foamy.

Meanwhile, mix the flour, salt, and remaining fructose in a large bowl. Add the remaining warm water and yeast mixture. Stir.

Turn out onto a floured surface and sprinkle with a little additional flour. Lightly oil your hands to prevent sticking. Knead the dough for 7 to 10 minutes, sprinkling with flour when necessary and adding the cheddar as you knead.

Place the dough in greased bowl, cover and let rise in warm place for 1½ to 2 hours.

Punch the dough down and let rise until double, about 45 minutes.

Punch down once more and place in a greased 9 x 5-inch loaf pan. Place in a cold oven. Place a pan of hot water in the oven, as well, and close the door. Let rise about 30 minutes or until the dough is above the rim of the pan.

Remove the hot water, being careful not to disturb the loaf. Turn the oven to 350 degrees and bake 45 to 50 minutes.

½ inch slice: Total Fat (g): 2
                Protein (g): 4
                Total Carbohydrates (g): 16
                Dietary Fiber (g): 3
                113 calories

Food Exchanges: Starch/Bread: 1, Fat: ½

Cinnamon Swirl Loaf

<u>Omit the cheese</u>, but follow above directions (for Whole Wheat Cheddar Bread) through the first rising.

During the first rising, mix *3 tablespoons ground cinnamon* with *3 tablespoons fructose*. Set aside.

After the first rising, punch the dough down. Roll out onto a lightly floured surface no wider than the width of the loaf pan you are using and no more than ½ inch thick.

Spread the surface with *2 tablespoons softened butter*. Sprinkle with the cinnamon mixture. Roll up jellyroll style. Pinch the ends to seal. Place in a greased loaf pan, with the seam side at the bottom.

Cover with a clean dishtowel; let rise and bake as directed.

½ inch slice: Total Fat (g): 2
                Protein (g): 3
                Total Carbohydrates (g): 20
                Dietary Fiber (g): 3
                99 calories

Food Exchanges: Starch/Bread: 1, Fat: ½, Other Carb: ½

Corn Bread
Especially nice with a hearty bowl of bean soup.

¼ cup fine wheat bran*
¼ cup soy flour
½ cup stone ground corn meal (blue corn meal is highest in fiber)
1 tablespoon baking powder
½ teaspoon salt
½ cup heavy cream
½ cup water
1 egg
1 tablespoon canola oil

Preheat the oven to 425 degrees.

Mix together the dry ingredients. Add the remaining ingredients and mix well.

Pour into a well-greased 8-inch casserole. Bake 20 to 25 minutes or until slightly brown on the top and the sides begin pulling away from pan. Cut into 2 inch squares.

Makes 16 (2 inch) squares. Serves 6 - 8.

1/8 recipe: Total Fat (g): 9
Protein (g): 3
Total Carbohydrates (g): 9
Dietary Fiber (g): 2
117 calories

Food Exchanges: Starch/Bread: ½, Lean Meat: ½, Fat: 1½

*Oat bran may be substituted.

Crispy Corn Sticks with Chilies

2/3 cup stone ground corn meal
1/3 cup fine wheat bran*
1 teaspoon salt
2 teaspoons baking powder
1 egg, beaten
1¼ cups water
1 tablespoon corn or canola oil
1 (4 ounce) can diced green chilies

Grease or spray corn-stick forms with non-stick cooking spray and place in the oven. Preheat the oven to 400 degrees.

Combine the dry ingredients in a medium bowl. Set aside.

In a small bowl, mix egg, water, oil, and chilies. Gently add to the dry ingredients; stir just until moistened.

Remove the pans carefully from the oven and place on a heatproof surface. Drop batter by spoonfuls into each corn-stick mold. Fill each about ¾ full. Return immediately to the oven and bake 15 to 20 minutes, until the tops are brown.

Makes 12 to 14 corn-sticks.

1/6 recipe: Total Fat (g): 4
          Protein (g): 3
          Total Carbohydrates (g): 14
          Dietary Fiber (g): 2
          94 calories

Food Exchanges: Starch/Bread: 1, Fat: ½

* Oat bran may be substituted.

Sun Dried Tomato & Olive Bread

2 cups whole wheat flour
½ cup soy flour
2 tablespoons flaxseed meal
½ cup grated parmesan cheese
1 teaspoon dried basil
½ teaspoon salt
1 tablespoon baking powder
1 (2.25 ounce) can sliced ripe olives, drained
½ cup sun dried olives, oil packed
2 eggs
1½ cup plain soy milk
1/3 cup olive oil

Preheat the oven to 425 degrees. Spray an 8-inch square pan with olive oil.

In a large bowl, combine the dry ingredients (first 7 ingredients). Set aside.

Slice or chop the sun dried tomatoes into smaller pieces. Combine with the drained olives. Set aside.

In a medium bowl, beat the eggs with the soy milk and oil until combined. Add this to the dry ingredients and mix with a large spoon just until well combined. Pour into the prepared pan and place in oven. Bake 30 minutes, until fragrant and the top begins to brown. A knife inserted in center will come out clean.

Makes 16 servings.

1 serving: Total Fat (g): 4
             Protein (g): 7
             Total Carbohydrates (g): 15
             Dietary Fiber (g): 4
             141 calories

Food Exchanges: Starch/Bread: 1, Lean Meat: ½, Fat: 1½

Basic Whole Wheat Rolls
It's easiest to make these ahead of time as refrigerator rolls.

1 package active dry yeast
¼ cup warm water (110 degrees)
1 cup milk, scalded
3 tablespoons fructose
¼ cup butter or coconut oil
1 teaspoon salt
3¼ cups whole wheat flour (fluff with spoon before measuring)
1 egg

Soften the yeast in the warm water.

Combine milk, fructose, butter, and salt. To save time, combine all in a small microwave-safe bowl and heat 2 minutes on high. Remove and stir until the shortening is melted. Pour into a large bowl. Cool to lukewarm. Add 1½ cups flour. Beat in the yeast and egg. Gradually add the remaining flour to form a soft dough, beating well. Place in a greased bowl, turning once to grease the surface. Cover and let rise in a warm place until double (1½ - 2 hours).

Turn out onto a lightly floured surface and shape as desired, placing on a greased baking sheet or in well-greased muffin tins. Cover and let the shaped rolls rise until double (30 to 45 minutes). Bake at 400 degrees for 12 to 15 minutes. Makes 2 dozen cloverleaf or 3 dozen parker house rolls.

Cloverleaf rolls
Shape dough into walnut-sized balls and place three balls in each greased muffin tin. Brush with butter and cover before rising.

Parkerhouse rolls
Roll the dough ¼ inch thick. Cut into circles with a biscuit cutter. Brush with butter, fold in half; then place on a greased baking sheet and cover to rise. Be sure to leave about one inch between rolls to leave room for expansion.

Refrigerator rolls
This dough may be made one to five days ahead. Make the basic whole-wheat roll dough. Do not let rise. Place in the refrigerator and take out 1½ hours before serving. Form into desired shape. Let rise in a warm place until doubled (about an hour). Bake as directed above.

1/12 recipe: Total Fat (g): 6 Protein (g): 6
                Total Carbohydrates (g): 29
                Dietary Fiber (g): 4
                181 calories

Food Exchanges: Starch/Bread: 1½, Fat: 1, Other Carb: ½

Cinnamon rolls

Mix 3 tablespoons ground cinnamon with 3 tablespoons fructose. Set aside.

After the first rising or after taking the chilled dough from the refrigerator (if you have made the dough ahead), roll the dough to ¼ inch thick. Brush with melted butter. Sprinkle with cinnamon sugar. Roll up as for a jellyroll. Seal the long edge. Then, slice with a sharp knife into rolls ½ inch thick. Place 1 inch apart on a baking sheet. Cover and let rise as directed in warm place. Bake at 400 degrees for 12 to 15 minutes.

Parmesan Pull-Apart Bread Balls

1 recipe for basic whole wheat rolls, prepared as refrigerator rolls, chilled at least 2 hours
1/3 cup butter, melted
1/3 cup grated Parmesan cheese

Grease a 10-inch tube pan (or spray with non-stick spray)

Form walnut-sized balls with the dough. Dip each in butter, then cheese, placing in the tube pan as you go.

Cover and let rise in warm place, about one hour or until doubled in size.

Bake 325 degrees for 25 to 30 minutes or until golden brown.

Serves 12 to 18.

1/18 of recipe: Total Fat (g): 8
Protein (g): 5
Total Carbohydrates (g): 20
Dietary Fiber (g): 3
Calories: 157

Food Exchanges: Starch/Bread: 1, Fat: 1½

Whole Grain Dry Bread Crumbs
Make ahead and store in airtight container.

6 slices whole grain bread

Lay the bread in single layer on cookie sheets. Bake 10 minutes in 300-degree oven for 10 minutes. Turn the slices over. Bake 5 additional minutes. Turn the oven off, leaving bread inside for 30 minutes. Remove and cool. Process or crush with rolling pin. Store in an airtight container.

Yield: about 1½ cups.

Soft Bread Crumbs

Place the whole grain bread slices in a freezer for 1 hour or until frozen. Remove and cut into ½ inch cubes with knife or place in food processor for finer crumbs. Each bread slice will make about ¼ cup of soft breadcrumbs.

Nutritional information will be found on bread package.

Basic Muffins
Add dried fruit or nuts for your own variations.

1 cup whole wheat flour*
1 tablespoon baking powder
¼ teaspoon salt
1 tablespoon fructose
¼ teaspoon cinnamon (ground)
⅓ cup plain soy milk
1 egg
2 tablespoons butter, melted (or canola oil)

Preheat oven to 375 degrees.

Combine the dry ingredients in a large bowl with a whisk

Measure the milk into a small bowl; add the egg and beat well. Pour the milk and egg mixture into the dry ingredients all at once and lightly mix, just till moistened. <u>Do not over-mix.</u>

Spoon the mixture into greased muffin tins or tins lined with paper muffin cups. Bake 20 minutes at 375 degrees.

1 muffin: Total Fat (g): 5
                Protein (g): 4
                Total Carbohydrates (g): 19
                Dietary Fiber (g): 3
                Calories: 132

Food Exchanges: Starch/Bread: 1, Fat: 1

Coconut-Apricot Muffins:
After mixing dry ingredients, stir in *¼-cup chopped dried apricots* and *1/3-cup unsweetened coconut*. Then, proceed as directed. <u>Be sure to use apricots that do not have added sugar.</u>

Be creative! Toss in nuts and other dried fruits, such as dried figs, cherries, or cranberries and create your own varieties.

Yield: 6 large muffins.

1 muffin: Total Fat (g): 7
                Protein (g): 5
                Total Carbohydrates (g): 23
                Dietary Fiber (g): 4
                Calories: 186

Food Exchanges: Starch/Bread: 1, Lean Meat: ½, Fruit: ½, Fat: 1 ½, Other Carb: ½

Spelt or kamut flour may be substituted.

Sweet Potato Muffins
This recipe, easily doubled, is fragrant with orange peel and sweet spices

¾ cup whole wheat flour *
¼ teaspoon salt
1 tablespoon baking powder
½ teaspoon ground cinnamon
¼ teaspoon ground ginger
¼ teaspoon ground nutmeg
¼ cup chopped nuts
2 tablespoons fructose or agave nectar **
½ cooked sweet potato (¼ cup after mashing)
1 large egg, slightly beaten
2 teaspoons finely grated orange zest (the orange part of the peel)
1/3 cup heavy cream + 3 tablespoons water

Preheat the oven to 400 degrees. Prepare the muffin tins (recipe makes 6 muffins) with paper liners or grease them with a non-stick spray or butter. Set aside.

In a medium bowl, combine the flour with the salt, baking powder, cinnamon, ginger, and nutmeg. Add the nuts and stir to coat the nuts with the flour mixture. Set aside.

In a small bowl, mash the sweet potato with a fork. The potato will be slightly lumpy. To the potato, add the sweetener, egg, grated orange zest, heavy cream and water.

Make a well in the center of the dry ingredients using a large spoon. Pour the sweet potato mixture into the well and stir with the spoon just until the dry ingredients are moistened. For a better texture, do not over-mix. Spoon the mixture into the prepared muffin tins. Place them in the preheated oven.
Bake the muffins 15 to 18 minutes, until a thin knife inserted in the center comes out clean and the tops are just beginning to brown.

Makes 6 muffins.

1 muffin (using fructose or agave):   Total Fat (g): 9
Protein (g): 4
Total Carbohydrates (g): 22
Dietary Fiber (g): 3
179 calories

Food Exchanges: Starch/Bread: 1, Fat: 1½, Other Carb: ½

If you want to bring the carb count lower, use the following substitutes. The texture is not as good as it is with only whole wheat, but the flavor is just as nice!

*Substitute ½-cup whole-wheat flour + ¼-cup defatted soy flour for ¾-cup whole-wheat flour.

**Substitute 2-tablespoons + 2-teaspoons Splenda for the fructose or agave nectar.

1 muffin: Total Fat (g): 9
Protein (g): 6
Total Carbohydrates (g): 13
Dietary Fiber (g): 3
153 calories

Food Exohangoo: Staroh/Broad: 1, Loan Moat: ¼, Fat: 1¼,

Blueberry Bran Muffins
Fragrant with a hint of orange peel and cinnamon

2 cups fresh blueberries
1½ cups all bran cereal with extra fiber (has less sugar)
1½ ups plain soy milk
1 large egg
1/3 cup canola oil
¾ cup Splenda (or alternative sweetener)
2 tablespoons freshly grated orange zest (colored peel)
1 teaspoon vanilla
1 cup whole wheat pastry flour
1 tablespoon baking powder
1 teaspoon cinnamon
¼ cups chopped pecans

Wash the blueberries, then remove the stems. Lay the berries on a paper towel to dry.

Preheat the oven to 375 degrees. Grease your muffin tins or line them with paper liners.

In a large mixing bowl, mix together the cereal and the soy milk; soak this mixture for about 15 minutes. Stir in the egg, oil, Splenda, orange zest, and vanilla.

In a separate bowl, combine the flour, baking powder, cinnamon and nuts. Gently stir in the blueberries.

All at once, add the dry ingredients to the cereal mixture. Gently stir, just until blended. Do not over-stir! Too much stirring destroys the light texture of muffins. Spoon the batter into greased or paper-lined muffin tins.

Bake the muffins for 25 minutes, until the cake tester inserted in the center of a muffin comes out clean.

Makes 18 muffins.

1 muffin: Total Fat (g): 8
            Protein (g): 3
            Total Carbohydrates (g): 12
            Dietary Fiber (g): 4

Food Exchanges: Starch/Bread: ½, Fat: 1½

Eight Grain Muffins
Taste and texture!

½ cup Seven Grain Cereal (a hot cereal - found in nutritional section or health food grocery store)
¾ cup plain soy milk
1 cup whole grain kamut flour*
½ teaspoon salt
2 teaspoons baking powder
2 tablespoons fructose
¼ teaspoon xanthan gum (optional - found with specialty flours -improves texture)
1 teaspoon cinnamon
¼ teaspoon nutmeg
½ cup chopped almonds, walnuts, or pecans
1 egg
½ cup oil

Preheat the oven to 350 degrees.

Combine the milk with the Seven Grain Cereal in a non-metal container. Heat 1 minute in the microwave and set aside. (Or heat the milk, then stir into the cereal and set aside.)

Grease the muffin tins or line with paper liners.

In a large bowl, combine the dry ingredients. Stir in the nuts.

In a medium bowl, combine the egg and oil. Combine the milk and egg mixture with the cereal mixture. Add to the dry ingredients, mixing gently, just until all ingredients are blended.

Drop into the prepared muffin cups, filling about 2/3 full.

Bake at 350 degrees for 22 minutes or until the tops are lightly browned.

Makes 9 medium sized muffins.

*Whole wheat or spelt flour may be substituted.

1 muffin: Total Fat (g): 18
　　　　　　　Protein (g): 7
　　　　　　　Total Carbohydrates (g): 26
　　　　　　　Dietary Fiber (g): 5

Food Exchanges: Lean Meat: ½, Fat: 3, Other Carb: ½

Perfect Biscuits
A Deep South Breakfast Basic

2 cups whole wheat flour* (fluff with spoon before measuring)
2 tablespoons baking powder
½ teaspoon salt
½ teaspoon cream of tartar
2 teaspoons fructose or alternative granulated sweetener
⅓ cup softened butter or coconut oil
2/3 cup plain soy milk

Preheat the oven to 450 degrees.

Mix the dry ingredients in a large bowl. Cut in the shortening until the mixture particles are the size of coarse crumbs. This is best done with a pastry cutter, but can also be done in a food processor. (If a processor is used, empty the mixture into a large bowl before proceeding.)

Make a well in the center of the flour mixture. Add the milk all at once. Stir with a fork just until the dough follows the fork around the bowl.

Lightly sprinkle a board, baking sheet, or flat (clean) counter top with flour. Turn the dough onto this. The dough should be soft. Knead the dough gently 10 to 12 times. (Press the dough in the center. Fold one outside edge to center and press again. Repeat 9 to 11 times.)

Roll or pat the dough to ½ inch thick. Dip a biscuit cutter (or edge of round glass) in flour. Cut straight through the dough, no twisting. Place the biscuits on an ungreased cookie sheet.

Bake 450 degrees for 10 to 12 minutes or till lightly browned.

Yield: about 12 medium biscuits

*Spelt or kamut flour may be substituted.

1 biscuit:	Total Fat (g): 8
	Protein (g): 3
	Total Carbohydrates (g): 17
	Dietary Fiber (g): 3
	Calories: 145

Food Exchanges: Starch/Bread: 1, Fat: 1½

Cinnamon Biscuits
Add 2 teaspoons ground cinnamon and one additional teaspoon of fructose with the dry ingredients. Brush tops with melted butter and sprinkle with cinnamon-fructose sugar, if desired.

Cinnamon-Fructose Sugar
2/3 cup fructose plus 1 tablespoon ground cinnamon, mixed and stored in an airtight container

Super Pancakes
A quick Saturday breakfast. Serve with sausage or bacon.

1 cup kamut flour*
2 teaspoons fructose or alternative granulated sweetener
1 tablespoon baking powder
¼ teaspoon salt
1¼ cup plain soy milk
1 egg
1 tablespoon canola oil
2 tablespoons chopped nuts (optional)
butter

Preheat and lightly oil a griddle or pan.

Mix the dry ingredients in a medium bowl. In a small bowl, mix the milk, egg, and oil. Add to the dry ingredients.

Pour by large tablespoons onto a greased hot griddle. Sprinkle with the nuts, if desired. Turn when the top begins to bubble and edges begin to dry. Brush with melted butter and serve hot.

Top with low carb syrup.

Alternative topping: Mix ¼ cup softened butter with ½ cup sugar-free marmalade or other sugar-free jam and spread lightly on each serving.

Makes 12 (3½ inch) pancakes.

*Whole wheat or spelt flour may be substituted.

4 pancakes: Total Fat (g): 12
               Protein (g): 11
               Total Carbohydrates (g): 38
               Dietary Fiber (g): 7
               285 calories

Food Exchanges: Starch/Bread: 2, Lean Meat: 1, Fat: 2, Other Carb: ½

Everyday Waffles

2 eggs, beaten
1½ cups plain soy milk
2 cups kamut or whole-wheat flour (fluff before measuring)
1 tablespoon baking powder
1 teaspoon salt
1 teaspoon cinnamon
½ cup plus 2 tablespoons butter, melted (or oil)

Preheat the waffle iron. Oil as directed by the manufacturer.

Combine the eggs and milk in a medium bowl.

In a separate bowl, combine flour, baking powder, salt, and cinnamon. Add to the egg mixture, stirring well. Mix in the melted butter. Spoon the batter into the waffle iron, being careful not to overfill. Cook 5 minutes or until brown and crisp. Repeat until all batter is cooked. Serve hot with butter and your favorite low carb syrup.

Makes 6 (6 inch) waffles

1 waffle: Total Fat (g): 23
    Protein (g): 10
    Total Carbohydrates (g): 31
    Dietary Fiber (g): 6
    349 calories

Food Exchanges: Starch/Bread: 2, Lean Meat: ½, Fat: 4 ½

Nut Waffles

Add ½ cup chopped nuts to the batter before baking.

1 waffle: Total Fat (g): 30
    Protein (g): 12
    Total Carbohydrates (g): 35
    Dietary Fiber (g): 6

Food Exchanges: Starch/Bread: 2, Lean Meat: ½, Fat: 5½

Sweet Potato Waffles

Add 1 small cooked, mashed sweet potato, combining with the milk and egg.

Makes 8 waffles.

1 waffle: Total Fat (g): 17
    Protein (g): 8
    Total Carbohydrates (g): 31
    Dietary Fiber (g): 6
    294 calories

Food Exchanges: Starch/Bread: 2, Lean Meat: ½, Fat: 3,

Optional topping: 1 cup whipping cream, whipped with 1-tablespoon fructose and ¼ teaspoon cinnamon.

Apple Bread

½ cup butter, softened
2/3 cup fructose or agave nectar (or ¾ cup granulated alternative sweetener)
2 eggs
1¾ cups kamut flour*
1 teaspoon ground flax seed
½ teaspoon salt
½ teaspoon baking powder
½ teaspoon baking soda
2 tablespoons buttermilk or soured milk**
1 cup coarsely chopped unpeeled apple (about 1 medium apple)
½ cup nuts
1 teaspoon vanilla

Preheat the oven to 350 degrees.

Cream the butter in a medium mixing bowl. Slowly add the fructose (or alternative sweetener); beat until light, fluffy, and lemon colored. Beat in the eggs.

Sift the dry ingredients together. Add to the creamed mixture alternately with milk, beginning and ending with dry ingredients. Stir in the remaining ingredients.

Grease a loaf pan. Spoon the batter into the pan. Bake 50 to 60 minutes or until the bread starts to pull away from the sides of the pan. Cool 5 minutes. Turn onto rack to finish cooling.

Makes 1 large or 3 small loaves.

1/8 recipe: Total Fat (g): 18
                   Protein (g): 7
                   Total Carbohydrates (g): 48
                   Dietary Fiber (g): 5
                   366 calories

Food Exchanges: Starch/Bread: 1½, Lean Meat: ½, Fruit: ½, Fat: 3½

Whole wheat or spelt flour may be substituted, but the flavor will not be as light.

To make soured milk, measure 2-tablespoons milk and add teaspoon vinegar. Let stand until ready to use.

Cranberry Nut Bran Bread
Everyone will enjoy this tasty bread.

1 cup dried cranberries, with no sugar added
1 cup boiling water
1 cup all bran cereal
1½ cups plain soy milk
1 egg
1½ cups whole wheat flour
1 tablespoon baking powder
½ teaspoon cinnamon
½ teaspoon salt
1 cup chopped walnuts
2 tablespoons butter, melted

In a medium bowl, pour the boiling water over the cranberries and set aside. Preheat the oven to 350 degrees.

In a small bowl, mix together the cereal, milk, and egg. Set aside.

In a food processor, place the flour, baking powder, cinnamon and salt. Process to mix.

Completely drain the cranberries, and then add them to the processor with the flour mixture. Process briefly to combine. Place the mixture in a large bowl. Stir in the walnuts. Add the cereal mixture, stirring just to mix. Stir in the melted butter. Pour into a large greased loaf pan.

Bake 1 hour at 350 degrees or until a wooden toothpick comes out clean when inserted in center.

Makes one 9-inch loaf.

½ inch slice: Total Fat (g): 6
              Protein (g): 4
              Total Carbohydrates (g): 11
              Dietary Fiber (g): 3
              107 calories

Food Exchanges: Starch/Bread: ½, Lean Meat: ½, Fat: 1

Dressings, Sauces & Dips

Spiced Whole Cranberry Sauce

This special sauce possesses the consistency of chutney. It is a lovely with poultry or pork, but also makes a pretty appetizer ladled over a block of cream cheese and served with whole grain crackers.

1/3 cup fructose or agave nectar
½ cup Splenda (or other granular alternative sweetener)
1 cup water
1 (12 ounce) package fresh or frozen cranberries
2 teaspoons freshly grated ginger
1/8 teaspoon ground cloves
1 - 3 individual packs of Splenda (optional)

In a medium saucepan, mix together the fructose and Splenda with water and stir to dissolve.

Rinse the cranberries under cool water; drain and add to the saucepan. Add the ginger and cloves and bring to a boil. Reduce the heat to very low; simmer for 10 minutes. Remove from the heat; pour into a small serving dish. Taste the sauce. If the sweetness is not to your liking, add the Splenda to taste. Cool the sauce. Refrigerate after cooling.

Makes about 2 cups.

¼ cup: Total Fat (g): 0
              Protein (g): 0
              Total Carbohydrates (g): 18
              Dietary Fiber (g): 2
              66 calories

Food Exchanges: Fruit: ½, Other Carb: ½

Jellied Cranberry Sauce

This natural jellied cranberry sauce has the consistency of applesauce, and is actually a true sauce, unlike the product that comes in a can!

1/3 cup fructose or agave nectar
½ cup Splenda (or other granular alternative sweetener)
1 cup water
1 (12 ounce) package fresh or frozen cranberries
2 teaspoons freshly grated ginger
1/8 teaspoon ground cloves
1 -2 individual packages of Splenda (optional)

In a medium saucepan, mix together the fructose and ½ cup Splenda with the water and stir to dissolve. Rinse the cranberries under cool water; drain and add to the saucepan. Add the ginger and cloves and bring to a boil. Reduce the heat to very low; simmer for 10 minutes. Remove from the heat.

Place a fine colander or sieve over a small bowl. Pour the cooked mixture into the sieve and press it through using the back of a large spoon. Only the peels of the cranberries should be left when you are finished. Discard the peel.

Taste the sauce and sweeten with additional Splenda, if desired. Cool; then pour into a small serving dish. Refrigerate after cooling.

Makes about 1 cup.

2 tablespoons: Total Fat (g): 0
Protein (g): 0
Total Carbohydrates (g): 18
Dietary Fiber (g): not available after removing skins of berries
66 calories

Food Exchanges: Fruit: ½, Other Carbs: 1

Balsamic Salad Dressing
Super as a salad dressing or as a poultry marinade.

½ cup balsamic vinegar
2 tablespoons lite soy sauce
2 tablespoons extra virgin olive oil
1 clove garlic, minced

Process all ingredients until blended.

Makes ¾ cup.

2 tablespoons:	Total Fat (g): 5
	Protein (g): trace
	Total Carbohydrates (g): 2
	Dietary Fiber (g): trace
	47 calories

Food Exchanges: Fat: 1

Bleu Cheese Vinaigrette
Perfect for green salads

1 small (3 ounces) package crumbled bleu cheese
1 cup canola oil
1/3 cup champagne or white wine vinegar
¼ teaspoon pepper
¼ teaspoon salt

Combine in a jar. Shake. Chill several hours before serving.

Makes 1-1/3 cups.

2 tablespoons:	Total Fat (g): 24
	Protein (g): 2
	Total Carbohydrates (g): 1
	Dietary Fiber (g): 0
	224 calories

Food Exchanges: Fat: 2½

Orange Poppyseed Dressing
Fabulous on a spinach salad with walnuts and sliced strawberries tossed in the bowl.

2 tablespoons fructose or agave nectar* (or equivalent below)
1½ teaspoon orange peel, finely grated
2 tablespoons orange juice
2 tablespoons white vinegar
1 tablespoon onion, finely chopped
1/3 cup canola oil
1 teaspoon poppyseed

Put first five ingredients in a processor. Slowly add oil through the hole, while processing. Blend. Remove cover and stir in poppy seed. Place in covered container and chill.

Makes ¾ cup.

2 tablespoons: Total Fat (g): 12
Protein (g): trace
Total Carbohydrates (g): 5 (Splenda), 7 (fructose or agave)
Dietary Fiber (g): trace
Calories: 124 (Splenda), 147 (fructose)

Food Exchanges: Fat: 2½, Other Carb: ½

*2 tablespoons + 2 teaspoons granulated alternative sweetener may be substituted.

Raspberry Vinaigrette
Wonderful served over fresh fruit or baby spinach for a light lunch!

½ cup canola oil
¼ cup champagne or white wine vinegar
2 teaspoons fructose or agave nectar (or alternative sweetener)
½ cup raspberries, pureed (strain, if desired)
2 tablespoons chopped walnuts
1 teaspoon finely diced onion
dash salt

Blend all ingredients in a blender or food processor. Store in a covered container in the refrigerator.

Makes 1-1/3 cups.

2 tablespoons: Total Fat (g): 12
Protein (g): trace
Total Carbohydrates (g): 3 (fructose), 1 (Splenda)
Dietary Fiber (g): 1
Calories: 114 (fructose), 110 (Splenda)

Food Exchanges: Fat: 2½

Tarragon Dressing
Great for grilling and marinating chicken.

2 tablespoons red wine vinegar
1 tablespoon Dijon mustard
1 tablespoon dried tarragon
1 clove garlic, minced
½ cup olive oil

Mix all ingredients with a whisk. Store in an airtight container.

Makes ¾ cup.

2 tablespoons: Total Fat (g): 18
Protein (g): trace
Total Carbohydrates (g): trace
Dietary Fiber (g): 1
165 calories

Food Exchanges: Fat: 3½

Spinach Salad Dressing
Pour over spinach, mushrooms, tomato wedges and crumbled feta cheese.

½ cup tarragon wine vinegar
¼ teaspoon dried tarragon
½ teaspoon salt
1/8 teaspoon pepper
2 teaspoons fructose, agave nectar, (or 3 teaspoons alternative sweetener)
1/8 teaspoon dried mustard
1 cup canola oil

Place the dry ingredients in a bowl. With a wire whisk, the beat vinegar into the spices. Add the oil and continue mixing until the oil is completely blended and is a light, creamy color.

Store in an airtight container and refrigerate.

Makes 1½ cups.

2 tablespoons: Total Fat (g): 18
Protein (g): trace
Total Carbohydrates (g): 2
Dietary Fiber (g): trace
166 calories

Food Exchanges: Fat: 3½

Quick Parmesan Sauce
Spoon over steamed broccoli or asparagus. An easy replacement for Hollandaise!

1/3 cup Parmesan cheese
1/3 cup sugar-free mayonnaise
1/3 cup sour cream

Mix all ingredients in a small bowl. After removing the cooked vegetables from the microwave or pot, drain and place in a serving bowl. Spread sauce over the top of the hot vegetable; then place a plate or lid over the bowl until ready to serve. The heat from the vegetables will melt the cheese and blend the sauce.

Makes 1 cup sauce.

1/6 recipe: Total Fat (g): 14
Protein (g): 2
Total Carbohydrates (g): 1
Dietary Fiber (g): 0
135 calories

Food Exchanges: Lean Meat: ½, Fat: 1½

BBQ Sauce
Always nice to have on hand.

2 tablespoons olive oil
1 small onion, finely minced
2 cloves garlic, crushed
3 tablespoons chili powder
1/3 cup red wine vinegar
1¼ cups water
2 tablespoons fructose or agave syrup (or 2 tablespoons + 2 teaspoons granular alternative)
2 tablespoons soy sauce
1 (6 ounces) can tomato paste
2 tablespoons yellow mustard
2 tablespoons lemon juice

Heat the oil in a saucepan. Add the onion and sauté until translucent. Add the garlic. Stir.

Add the chili powder, vinegar, water, fructose, soy sauce, and tomato paste. Mix and simmer for 30 minutes.

Add the mustard and lemon juice. Simmer for 15 additional minutes. Store in a sealed glass jar or keep in an airtight container in refrigerator.

Makes 2½ cups sauce.

1/4 cup: Total Fat (g): 3
Protein (g): 1
Total Carbohydrates (g): 11
Dietary Fiber (g): 2
65 calories

Food Exchanges: Vegetable: 1, Fat: ½, Other Carb: ½

Tangy Barbecue Sauce
A quick sauce that's great for grilling!

1 cup Dijon or seeded mustard
½ cup olive oil
½ teaspoon soy sauce

Combine all ingredients in a medium bowl with a wire whisk. Refrigerate until ready to use. Especially nice for pork and lamb.

To use, brush the meat with sauce and grill as desired.

Makes 2 cups sauce.

1/4 cup: Total Fat (g): 15
               Protein (g): 1
               Total Carbohydrates (g): 2
               Dietary Fiber (g): 1
               142 calories

Food Exchanges: Fat: 3

Salad, Relish & Slaw

Cranberry Relish
A holiday favorite!

2 cups fresh cranberries
2 oranges
2 apples, cored
1 lemon
¾ cup fructose or agave syrup
¼ cup Splenda (or alternative granular sweetener)

Rinse and drain the cranberries, removing stems as needed.

Grate all zest (colored part of peel only) from the lemon and oranges. Place the zest in a food processor.

Peel the lemon and orange and remove all seeds. Add the citrus fruit to the processor.

Wash the apple, remove the core, and then cut into chunks. Add to the processor. Add the fructose and Splenda, then process until mixture is finely chopped and evenly mixed. Refrigerate.

Store in an airtight container.

Makes about 3 cups.

2 tablespoons:	Total Fat (g): trace
	Protein (g): trace
	Total Carbohydrates (g): 13
	Dietary Fiber (g): 1

Food Exchanges: Fruit: ½, Other Carb: 1½

Tomato Avocado Relish
Try it on a grilled burger in place of other condiments!

3 ripe tomatoes
1 avocado
¼ cup red onion, diced
½ teaspoon salt
juice of 1 lime

If desired, peel the tomatoes. Cut into quarters and remove the seeds and pulp. Dice and place in a small bowl.

Peel and dice the avocado. Toss with the diced tomatoes. Add the diced onion, salt and lime juice. Toss and refrigerate at least one hour.

Serves 4 - 5.

1/5 recipe: Total Fat (g): 6
Protein (g): 2
Total Carbohydrates (g): 8
Dietary Fiber (g): 2
86 calories

Food Exchanges: Vegetable: 1, Fat: 1

Apple Cherry Salad

Cherries and apples are temperate, low glycemic fruits that everyone can enjoy. This salad also provides a hearty serving of essential fatty acids in the walnuts and their oil

1 tablespoon mayonnaise, sugar free if possible*
1 tablespoon walnut oil
1 tablespoon white wine vinegar
1 teaspoon agave syrup (or 1 packet Splenda)

2 large apples (about 3 cups diced)
¼ cup dried cherries, no sugar added
½ cup walnuts
¼ cup freshly grated (or dried) unsweetened coconut

In a cup or a small bowl, combine the mayonnaise, walnut oil, white wine vinegar and sweetener, beating the mixture together with a fork or small whisk. If using dried coconut, rather than fresh, add the coconut at this time so that it can absorb moisture from the dressing. Refrigerate the dressing until you are ready to use it.

Peel, core, and dice the apples. Place them in a medium bowl. Add the dried cherries, nuts, and coconut. Pour the dressing over the salad ingredients and toss them together to coat the fruit. Place in a pretty serving dish and refrigerate the salad until ready to serve.

Serves 8.

1 serving: Total Fat (g): 9
              Protein (g): 1
              Total Carbohydrates (g): 12
              Dietary Fiber (g): 2
              120 calories

Food Exchanges: Lean Meat: ½, Fruit: ½, Fat: 1½

Apple Salad with Cranberry Confetti Dressing

Try this little salad recipe for pretty and festive dish. Quick and easy to make, it looks nice on a buffet, for ladies luncheon or to take as a healthy covered dish to your next "pot luck" occasion.

Cranberry Confetti Dressing

1 tablespoon olive oil
¾ cup freshly squeezed orange juice
1 cup fresh cranberries, washed and drained
2 teaspoons fructose, agave nectar or whey low (or 3 teaspoons Splenda)
3 ounces cream cheese
½ teaspoon freshly grated orange zest (the orange part of the peel)

Salad Ingredients

¼ cup diced celery
2 apples, peeled, cored and diced (about 2 cups)
1 (11 ounce) can mandarin oranges, drained
½ cup chopped walnuts

Combine all the dressing ingredients in a blender or food processor, using the sharp blade. Process until well blended. The mixture will look smooth and pink. The cranberry peel will have broken apart into confetti-sized pieces. Place the dressing in a glass, plastic or ceramic container and refrigerate.

Drain the oranges and place in a medium-size serving bowl. Chop the walnuts and add. Dice the celery and add them to the oranges; then core the apples, peeling if desired. Dice the apples and add to the oranges; toss the fruit and nuts together gently. Pour the dressing over all and toss to coat the fruit and nuts. Refrigerate until ready to serve. This salad will keep well for a day or so in the refrigerator and can be made the day before serving.

Makes about 8 servings.

1 serving: Total Fat (g): 9
Protein (g): 2
Total Carbohydrates (g): 32 (fructose); 27 (Splenda)
Dietary Fiber (g): 5
151 calories (fructose), 145 calories (Splenda)

Food Exchanges: Lean Meat: ½, Fruit 1½, Fat 1½, Other Carb: ½ (with fructose)

Broccoli Pear Salad
A yummy salad, with a sweetly spiced dressing.

Sweetly Spiced Dressing
1/3 cup canola oil
2 tablespoons Champaign or white wine vinegar
1 tablespoon sherry
½ teaspoon freshly grated ginger
¼ teaspoon allspice
1 teaspoon agave nectar (or 1 packet alternative sweetener)

Salad
2 cups broccoli, cut into bite-sized pieces
½ cup walnuts
¼ cup red onion, diced
1-2 ripe pears, cut into thin slices (about 1¾ cup after slicing)

Mix all the dressing ingredients in a small container or jar. Shake or whisk to combine.

In your serving bowl, place all the salad ingredients (broccoli, onion, walnuts, and pears) Pour the dressing over and toss gently to coat.

Serves 8.

1 serving: Total Fat (g): 14
               Protein (g): 3
               Total Carbohydrates (g): 9
               Dietary Fiber (g): 2
               162 calories

Food Exchanges: Vegetable: ½, Fruit: ½, Fat: 2½

Broccoli Salad with Oranges

Broccoli is terrific for regulating blood sugar. Try this simple, colorful and refreshing salad, sweetened with a sprinkling of oranges.

1 whole stalk broccoli
½ red onion, diced
1 small can mandarin oranges, drained

Salad dressing
1 tablespoon Splenda or fructose
1/3 cup safflower or canola oil
1½ teaspoons finely grated fresh orange peel
juice of 1 orange
1 tablespoon white wine vinegar

Remove the flowerettes from the head of the broccoli; wash and drain. Cut into small, bite-sized flowerettes. Place in a large bowl.

Clean and peel the stems of the broccoli as needed. Cut into 1- inch chunks. Place in a processor and chop until evenly chopped and about pea-sized. Add to the bowl. Add the diced onion and the drained mandarin slices.

In a small bowl, combine the dressing ingredients and whisk until blended. Pour over the broccoli mixture and gently toss together. Refrigerate.

Serves 4 to 5.

1/4 recipe: Total Fat (g): 8
                Protein (g): 1
                Total Carbohydrates (g): 8
                Dietary Fiber (g): 1

Food Exchanges: Vegetable: ½, Fat: ½

Fruited Slaw

This delightful slaw is best made a day ahead, giving the fruit flavors time to develop! Refreshing, healthy and nice for a crowd, this recipe keeps well for a day or two in the refrigerator.

1 (8 ounce) can crushed pineapple in its own juice
½ cup dried cranberries
3 tablespoons white wine vinegar
1/3 cup mayonnaise
2 teaspoons Splenda or 2 packets powdered stevia
½ head cabbage, shredded (about 4 cups)
1 apple, peeled, cored and shredded (about 1 cup)

Drain the juice from the pineapple into a blender or food processor. Reserve the pineapple separately.

To the juice, add cranberries, vinegar, mayonnaise, and Splenda (or stevia). Process the mixture for about 30 seconds, to break up the cranberries, then pour all into a large bowl. Add the reserved pineapple to the bowl.

Shred the cabbage and apple, then remove to the large bowl. With a large spoon, mix all together and refrigerate until ready to serve.

Makes 10 servings.

1 serving: Total Fat (g): 6
           Protein (g): 1
           Total Carbohydrates (g): 7
           Dietary Fiber (g): 1
           81 calories

Food Exchanges: Vegetable: ½, Fruit: ½, Fat: ½

Pecan Apricot Slaw

This slaw holds together well when served using an ice cream scoop and placed on a small lettuce leaf. Garnish with a slice of dried apricot!

Slaw

3 cups shredded or finely chopped cabbage
½ cup onion, cut into chunks
1 rib celery, cut into 1 inch pieces
1 cup pecans

Place the shredded cabbage into a large bowl. Set aside. Place the remaining ingredients in a food processor and process until chopped to desired consistency. Add to the bowl with the cabbage.

Dried Apricot Dressing

1/3 cup white wine or Champaign vinegar
1/3 cup extra virgin olive oil
1 tablespoon agave nectar (or 1 tablespoon + 1 teaspoon Splenda)
1 tablespoon lemon juice
2 tablespoons mayonnaise
1 cup dried apricots, cup in half

Place all dressing ingredients in the food processor or a blender. Process until the apricots are finely chopped. Pour into the bowl with the slaw ingredients. Mix and refrigerate, tightly covered. Serve cold. Very nice to make ahead of time; keeps well for several days.

Serves 10.

1 serving (using agave or fructose):   Total Fat (g): 17
Protein (g): 1
Total Carbohydrates (g): 6
Dietary Fiber (g): 2
180 calories

Food Exchanges: Vegetable: ½, Fat: 3

Summer Blueberry Salad

Cool, delicious and creamy. This refreshing salad was created by my mother-in law and is perfect for a family gathering.

4 cups fresh blueberries
1 (0.3) ounce package lemon sugar-free jello
2 (8 ounce) cans unsweetened pineapple tidbits, well-drained
8 ounces cream cheese, softened
8 ounces sour cream
1 cup chopped walnuts

Place the jello in a 2-cup measuring cup. Add the boiling water to the 1-cup mark and dissolve thoroughly. Add the ice cubes to equal about 1¾ cups total and stir until melted.

Spread the blueberries across the bottom of a large (2-quart) casserole dish. Pour the jello mixture over the top and refrigerate until set, about an hour.

Mix the remaining ingredients together, then spread over the congealed blueberries. Refrigerate until ready to serve.

Serves up to 24.

1 serving: Total Fat (g): 32
                Protein (g): 8
                Total Carbohydrates (g): 8
                Dietary fiber (g): 1
                341 calories

Food Exchanges: Lean Meat: 1, Fruit ½, Fat: 6

Spinach Salad with Strawberry Poppyseed Dressing
A perfect pleasure while watching your carbohydrates! Try this salad with grilled fish or your favorite chicken dish.

Strawberry Poppyseed Dressing
1 cup sliced fresh strawberries
¼ cup red wine vinegar
1 tablespoon agave syrup (nectar)(or 1 tbsp + 1 tsp Splenda or alternative sweetener)
1 teaspoon poppyseeds
½ teaspoon dry mustard
½ cup canola oil

Blend all ingredients with a hand blender, blender or food processor. Refrigerate.

Makes 1 cup dressing.

Salad Ingredients
5 cups torn fresh spinach, washed and dried
1½ cups sliced fresh strawberries
1 cup sliced celery (about 2 ribs)
2 spring onions, thinly sliced

Place the salad ingredients in a serving bowl. Add about half the dressing just before serving and toss. Refrigerate remaining dressing for later.

Serves 4.

2 tablespoons dressing: Total Fat (g): 15
Protein (g): 0
Total Carbohydrates (g): 4
Dietary Fiber (g): 0
138 calories

Food Exchanges: Fat: 2½

1 serving salad ingredients (without dressing):   Total Fat: trace
Protein (g): 2
Total Carbohydrates (g): 6
Dietary Fiber (g): 3
32 calories

Exchanges: Vegetable: ½, Fruit: ½

White Bean Salad
Great with grilled tuna or chicken and whole-grain bread.

1 cup dried, uncooked white beans <u>or</u> 2 (15½ ounce) cans navy beans, drained & rinsed
2 tablespoons olive oil
1 cup finely shredded spinach
2 tomatoes, quartered

2 tablespoons Balsamic vinegar
½ teaspoon salt
¼ teaspoon dried basil
dash black pepper

One day ahead, soak and cook beans according to package directions. Drain. Mix with oil and refrigerate. If canned beans are used, drain, rinse, then mix with oil and proceed.

Before serving, combine the spices with the vinegar. Toss together with the beans and spinach. Arrange tomato wedges around the perimeter of the dish. Place the salad in the center to serve.

Yield: 4 servings

1 serving: Total Fat (g): 7
Protein (g): 12
Total Carbohydrates (g): 32
Dietary Fiber (g): 13
250 calories

Food Exchanges: Starch/Bread: 2, Lean Meat: ½, Fat: 1½

Marinated Tomatoes & Cucumbers
Luscious, vine-ripe tomatoes and garden-ripe cucumbers team up for a refreshing summer side dish.

Salad Ingredients
2 medium cucumbers
2 ripe, medium sized tomatoes
2 spring onions

Dressing
¼ cup extra virgin olive oil
¼ cup white wine vinegar
1/8 teaspoon salt
¼ teaspoon dried basil
1/8 teaspoon dried mustard

Young, firm cucumbers make the best slices, before the seeds inside are well developed. If using fresh cucumbers from the garden, there is no need to peel. If using waxed cucumbers from the supermarket, you might want to peel them for improved taste.

Wash the cucumbers and slice into thin slices. Place into your serving bowl.

Wash the tomatoes. If desired, peel, but it is not necessary. Cut the tomato in half, then in quarters and discard the seedy pulp and woody stem area. Dice the remaining tomato. Add to the cucumbers.

Wash, and then slice the spring onions. Add to the cucumbers and tomatoes and set the bowl aside.

In a small bowl or jar, mix together the dressing ingredients and quickly stir or shake to blend. Pour over the tomatoes and cucumbers. Toss gently and refrigerate, covered, until ready to serve.

Serves 4 to 6.

1/6 recipe: Total Fat (g): 9
Protein (g): 1
Total Carbohydrates (g): 5
Dietary Fiber (g): 1
104 calories

Food Exchanges: Vegetable: 1, Fat: 2

Marinated Veggie Toss

Onions, broccoli and mushrooms are terrific foods to help regulate your insulin. Try this easy and tasty dish!

Salad Ingredients

1½ pounds broccoli flowerettes
1 small red onion, sliced into thin strips
1 pound mushrooms, sliced
1 (4.5 ounce.) jar pimento stuffed olives, drained
1 (3 ounce.) can sliced ripe olives, drained

Dressing

½ cup white wine vinegar
½ cup extra virgin olive oil
½ teaspoon basil
½ teaspoon oregano
1/8 teaspoon salt
1 small clove garlic, crushed

Place the vegetables in a large bowl.

Mix the dressing ingredients in a jar and shake them together or mix in a bowl with a whisk. Pour over the vegetables and gently mix. Marinate at least 2 hours or overnight.

1/6 recipe: Total Fat (g): 22
           Protein (g): 2
           Total Carbohydrates (g): 9
           Dietary Fiber (g): 6
           266 calories

Food Exchanges: Vegetable: 1, Fat: 4½

Mediterranean Broccoli Salad

Easy to make ahead, rich in monounsaturated fat, everyone will enjoy this colorful and tasty salad.

Dressing

½ cup extra virgin olive oil
¼ cup balsamic vinegar
1/8 teaspoon oregano
¼ teaspoon salt

Salad Ingredients

2 cups broccoli florets
1 (4 ounce.) can sliced black olives, drained
1 (7 ounce) jar roasted red peppers, drained and diced
½ cup red onions, thinly sliced
1 (4 ounce) package crumbled feta cheese

Combine the dressing ingredients in a jar or bowl and set aside.

In a salad bowl, combine the broccoli with all other ingredients. Whisk together the dressing ingredients and pour over the vegetables. Gently stir to combine. Refrigerate until ready to serve.

Serves 8.

1 serving: Total Fat (g): 18
  Protein (g): 3
  Total Carbohydrates (g): 5
  Dietary Fiber (g): 3
  191 calories

Food Exchanges: Vegetable: ½, Lean Meat: ½, Fat: 3 ½

Marinated Tomatoes
The taste of summer in Italy

3 large ripe tomatoes, quartered
¼ cup onion, minced
1/3 cup olive oil
¼ cup red wine vinegar
1 clove garlic, crushed
1 teaspoon dried basil
½ teaspoon oregano

Arrange the tomatoes and onion in a shallow bowl.

Mix the olive oil, vinegar, basil, and oregano. Pour over the tomatoes and onions. Cover and marinate 3 hours.

Serves 4 to 5.

1/4 recipe   Total Fat (g): 18
Protein (g): 1
Total Carbohydrates (g): 6
Dietary Fiber (g): 1
187 calories

Food Exchanges: Vegetable: 1, Fat: 3½

Marinated Asparagus
Substitute 1 pound of asparagus for tomatoes in the above recipe.

1/4 recipe: Total Fat (g): 18
Protein (g): 2
Total Carbohydrates (g): 5
Dietary Fiber (g): 1
181 calories

Food Exchanges: Vegetable: 1, Fat: 3½

Avocado Salad
Avocados are packed with nutrition.

Bacon Dressing
4 slices bacon, cooked, drained, and crumbled
1/3 cup extra virgin olive oil
¼ cup red wine vinegar
dash Tabasco sauce
½ teaspoon salt
1/8 teaspoon oregano
1/8 teaspoon ground black pepper
dash ground cayenne pepper

Salad Ingredients
2 medium avocados, peeled and cut into slices
2 medium tomatoes, cut into wedges
1 small bunch green onions with tops, sliced lengthwise with roots removed
2 to 3 cups shredded red leaf lettuce

Mix the bacon, olive oil, vinegar, Tabasco, salt, oregano and ground peppers in a medium bowl. Peel the avocadoes. Cut in half, lengthwise; then slice each avocado into about 8 slices. Add to the bowl and toss to coat. Cover and refrigerate at least one hour.

When ready to serve, toss the shredded lettuce and green onions together. Place on a serving platter. Remove the avocados from the salad dressing, reserving the dressing. Arrange the avocado slices and tomato wedges over the top of the lettuce. Serve with the salad dressing on the side or drizzle the platter with the dressing in which the avocados had been marinated and serve immediately.

Serves 4 to 6.

1/4 recipe: Total Fat (g): 37
Protein (g): 5
Total Carbohydrates (g): 12
Dietary Fiber (g): 4
379 calories

Food Exchanges: Lean Meat: ½, Vegetable: 1, Fruit: ½, Fat: 7

Avocado Tomato Salad with Lime Vinaigrette
Easy and excellent accompaniment with Tex-Mex dishes!

Lime Vinaigrette
juice of 1 lime (about 2 tablespoons)
¼ cup white wine vinegar
1/3 cup extra virgin olive oil
1 teaspoon grated onion
1/8 teaspoon dried oregano

Mix all ingredients and store, covered, in refrigerator. Before serving, whip with fork or whisk.

Salad Ingredients
2 medium avocados, slightly soft to touch
2-3 cups shredded romaine lettuce
1 (5½ ounces) can sliced black olives
2 medium tomatoes, cut into wedges

Peel the avocados. Cut in half, lengthwise; then slice each avocado into about 8 wedges. Place in a small bowl and toss with about ¼ cup dressing. Set aside.

In the serving bowl, toss the lettuce and olives together. Arrange the avocados and tomatoes on top and serve with the remaining dressing.

Serves 4 - 6.

1/4 recipe: Total Fat (g): 38
Protein (g): 3
Total Carbohydrates (g): 15
Dietary Fiber (g): 5
387 calories

Food Exchanges: Vegetable: ½, Fruit: ½, Fat: 7½

Avocado Shrimp Salad
Perfect for a lovely luncheon.

¼ cup white wine vinegar
1 cup fresh cilantro, loosely measured
½ teaspoon salt
¼ teaspoon pepper
2 ripe avocados
1 medium tomato
1 tablespoon grated onion
1 pound medium shrimp, cooked and peeled
½ cup sugar-free mayonnaise
4 to 5 cups mixed greens, torn for salad

Puree the vinegar, cilantro, salt and pepper together in a food processor or blender. Set aside.

Peel and dice the avocados. Pour the vinegar mixture over the avocados and toss gently to coat the avocados.

Dice the tomato, removing and discarding the seeded pulp with your fingers. Add the diced tomato to the avocados. Add the onion, shrimp and mayonnaise. Mix gently and refrigerate until ready to serve.

To serve, place the torn greens on the bottom of the platter. Top with the shrimp salad.

Serves 4 to 6.

1/4 recipe: Total Fat (g): 41
                      Protein (g): 28
                      Total Carbohydrates (g): 13
                      Dietary Fiber (g): 5
                      497 calories

Food Exchanges: Lean Meat: 3 ½, Vegetable: 1, Fruit: ½, Fat: 5

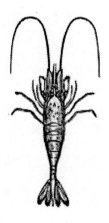

Mexican Bean Salad
Quick and easy!

1 (15 ounce) can white beans, drained and rinsed
1 (15 ounce) can dark red kidney beans, drained and rinsed
1 cup celery, thinly sliced
½ cup onion, diced
¼ cup apple cider vinegar
⅓ cup salsa
2 tablespoons olive oil
1 yellow pepper, seeded and thinly sliced
Lettuce and fresh cilantro (optional)

Combine all the ingredients in a medium bowl. Chill and serve. This salad looks nice when served on a bed of lettuce and garnished with cilantro.

Serves 6.

1 serving: Total Fat (g): 5
                Protein (g): 10
                Total Carbohydrates (g): 31
                Dietary Fiber (g): 9
                220 calories

Food Exchanges: Starch/Bread: 1½, Lean Meat: ½, Vegetable: 1, Fat: 1

Mediterranean Chicken Salad
This salad makes a nice dish for a Sunday picnic.

Dressing
½ cup olive oil
¼ cup balsamic vinegar
1/8 teaspoon oregano
½ teaspoon salt

Salad Ingredients
2 cups cooked chicken, cut into cubes
1 (4 ounces) can sliced black olives, drained
1 (7 ounces) jar roasted red peppers, drained and diced
1 (7½ ounces) jar marinated artichoke hearts (not drained)
1 (4 ounces) package crumbled feta cheese

In a small bowl, combine the olive oil, vinegar, oregano and salt.

In a medium bowl, place all the remaining ingredients. Whip the dressing ingredients together with a fork, and then pour over the chicken mixture. Gently toss and refrigerate until served.

Serves 4.

1 serving: Total Fat (g): 42
            Protein (g): 28
            Total Carbohydrates (g): 11
            Dietary Fiber (g): 4
            530 calories

Food Exchanges: Lean Meat: 3½, Vegetable: 1½, Fat: 7 ½

German Sweet Potato Salad
Divine with grilled chicken or a hamburger!

8 slices bacon
¼ cup olive oil
4 medium sweet potatoes, peeled and sliced
1 cup onion, thinly sliced
2 teaspoons fructose (or 3 teaspoons alternative granular sweetener)
4 teaspoons whole-wheat flour
2/3 cup water
2/3 cup red wine vinegar

Cook the bacon, reserving the drippings. Crumble the cooked bacon and set aside.

Place the olive oil in a skillet. Heat over medium heat, and cook the sweet potatoes, turning each slice once. Remove with a slotted spoon as soon as the potatoes are tender, about 2 minutes. Place in a serving dish.

Remove excess oil from the skillet. Add 1 tablespoon bacon drippings, then the onions. Saute until tender. Remove and place the onions in the dish with the potatoes. Add the crumbled bacon.

To the skillet, add 1½ tablespoons bacon drippings. Stir in the fructose and flour. Add the water and the vinegar, stirring with a wire whisk, until the mixture is thickened. Pour over the potatoes and onions and gently toss.

Serves 6.

1 serving: Total Fat (g): 13
Protein (g): 5
Total Carbohydrates (g): 28
Dietary Fiber (g): 3
243 calories

Food Exchanges: Starch/Bread: 1½, Lean Meat: ½, Vegetable: ½, Fat: 1

Marinated Zucchini Salad

Feta Dressing
¼ cup extra virgin olive oil
¼ cup white wine vinegar
1 small clove garlic, crushed
¼ teaspoon dried basil
¼ cup crumbled feta cheese

Salad Ingredients
3 small zucchini, thinly sliced
2 medium ripe tomatoes, sliced into thin wedges
1 (2¼ ounces) can black olives, drained
Leaf lettuce and additional tomato, cut into wedges (optional)

Mix the olive oil, vinegar, garlic, and basil, and feta cheese in a small bowl. Set aside.

Place the zucchini, tomatoes, and olives in the bowl. Pour the dressing over the vegetables and gently toss. Refrigerate one hour or more.

To serve, line a serving bowl with lettuce leaves and spoon the vegetables on top. If desired, garnish the dish with additional tomato slices.

Serves 6 to 8.

1/6 recipe: Total Fat (g): 12
Protein (g): 2
Total Carbohydrates (g): 6
Dietary Fiber (g): 2
133 calories

Food Exchanges: Vegetable: 1, Fat: 2

Mixed Rice Salad
A sweet, spicy taste.

Salad Ingredients
½ cup wild rice
½ cup brown rice
2½ cups water
¼ cup chopped celery
¼ cup chopped walnuts
¼ cup chopped cherries

Cardamom Dressing
2 tablespoons extra virgin olive oil
2 teaspoons fructose or agave syrup
½ teaspoon ground cardamom
½ teaspoon vanilla

Bring the water to a boil. Add the wild rice; cover and simmer over low heat for 10 minutes. Add the brown rice; cover and continue cooking for 50 minutes. Remove from heat and cool. Drain, if necessary. Refrigerate.

To make the dressing, combine the olive oil, fructose, cardamom, and vanilla. Set aside.

Toss the celery, walnuts, cherries and dressing with rice. Serve chilled or at room temperature.

Serves 6 to 8.

1/6 recipe: Total Fat (g): 8
Protein (g): 5
Total Carbohydrates (g): 31
Dietary Fiber (g): 2
213 calories

Food Exchanges: Starch/Bread: 1½, Fruit: ½, Fat: 1½

Artichoke Rice Salad
Pretty, nutritious, and delicious.

Salad Ingredients
2 (6 ounce) jars marinated artichoke hearts, undrained
2¼ cups brown rice, cooked and cooled (¾ cup raw rice & 1 ½ cups liquid)
2 cups chicken, cooked and cubed
1 (3 ounce) jar pimentos, drained

Yogurt Curry Dressing
½ cup mayonnaise
½ cup plain yogurt
1½ teaspoons curry powder
1½ teaspoons black pepper

Drain the artichokes, reserving the liquid. Use the marinade to cook the rice, adding additional water to 1½ cups. Cool the rice to room temperature. Prepare the dressing while the rice is cooling.

Combine the mayonnaise, yogurt, curry powder and pepper. Refrigerate.

After the rice is cooled, combine the artichoke hearts, chicken and pimentos with the rice. Toss with the dressing. Chill for at least 2 hours.

Makes 8 servings.

1 serving: Total Fat (g): 17
Protein (g): 14
Total Carbohydrates (g): 18
Dietary Fiber (g): 3
273 calories

Food Exchanges: Starch/Bread: 1½, Lean Meat: 1½, Vegetable: ½, Fat: 1½

Sweet Potato Salad
Delicious! Very nice to take for covered dish meals.

1/3 cup dried figs
4 medium sweet potatoes
½ cup mayonnaise
¼ cup unsweetened shredded coconut
1 tablespoon fructose (or 1 tablespoon + 1 teaspoon Splenda)
1/3 cup nuts, chopped

Place the figs in a small bowl. Cover with hot water and set aside.

Cut the sweet potatoes into 1-inch cubes. Cover with water. Boil 15 minutes or until tender, but not overdone. Drain, rinse with cold water and drain again. Place in a large bowl. Cool to room temperature.

Thoroughly drain the figs and chop into small pieces.

To make dressing, mix the mayonnaise with the fructose and coconut. Set aside.

Add the dressing, nuts, and figs to the sweet potatoes. Mix gently and refrigerate 2 hours or overnight.

Serves 6 to 8.

1/6 recipe: Total Fat (g): 22
Protein (g): 3
Total Carbohydrates (g): 34
Dietary Fiber (g): 5
322 calories

Food Exchanges: Starch/Bread: 1½, Fruit: ½, Fat: 2½

Soup

Lentil Soup
Easy and filling. Nice with high fiber cornbread and salad.

2 cups lentils, rinsed and drained
4 (14½ ounce) cans beef or chicken broth*
1 medium onion, chopped
1 stalk celery, chopped
1 tablespoon olive oil
1 carrot, thinly sliced (Carrots do not increase the glycemic value of lentil soup!)

Place the lentils and broth in a large saucepan. Bring to boil and simmer.

Sauté the onion and celery in the oil until tender and the onion is translucent. Add these vegetables to the soup along with the thinly sliced carrot. Simmer 1½ to 2 hours. Add additional water during the cooking, if desired, for thinner consistency.

Serves 8.

*With red lentils, use chicken broth.

 With dark lentils, use beef broth.

1 serving: Total Fat (g): 2
              Protein (g): 18
              Total Carbohydrates (g): 31
              Dietary Fiber (g): 15
              236 calories

Food Exchanges: Starch/Bread: 2, Lean Meat: 1 ½, Vegetable: ½, Fat: ½

Beef & Lentil Soup with Okra

Hearty, filling, and bursting with protein and fiber, this soup is even better the next day.

2 teaspoons olive oil
1 pound lean stew beef, cut into bite-sized cubes
1 medium onion, chopped (about 1 cup)
2 ribs celery, thinly sliced (about 1 cup)
1 (14.5 ounce) beef broth
1 (10 ounce) package frozen sliced okra
1 cup lentils
1 teaspoon salt (to taste)
¼ teaspoon black pepper

In a large soup pot or Dutch oven, heat the oil over medium heat. Add the stew beef, celery and onion. Sauté until the onion is tender and translucent.

Add the beef broth, 2 cans of water and the okra. Bring to a boil; then reduce to a simmer.

Place the lentils in a fine strainer and quickly rinse with cold water. Add the lentils and the seasonings to the soup. The lentils may stick together. Just use a fork to separate them as you add them. Stir the soup.

Cook over very low heat for 1½ to 2 hours, stirring and adding water as needed.

Serves 8.

1 serving: Total Fat (g): 4
                Protein (g): 24
                Total Carbohydrates (g): 19
                Dietary Fiber (g): 9
                218 calories

Food Exchanges: Starch/ Bread: ½, Lean Meat: 3, Vegetable: 1

Gumbo Ya Ya with Andouille Sausage

What could be better on a chilly day than a special pot of gumbo? If you like it hot and spicy, this dish is for you! But, for the "false alarm" version, use a milder sausage.

3 tablespoons olive oil
¼ cup whole wheat flour
2 cups chopped onions
1 cup chopped celery
3 cloves garlic, minced
½ cup chopped bell pepper
2 (14.5 ounce) cans chicken broth
2 cups sliced okra
1 (14.5 ounce) can diced tomatoes
1 cup lentils (yellow ones look nicer)
1 (10 ounce) package andouille sausage, diced*
salt to taste
1 teaspoon Tabasco sauce
1 teaspoon gumbo file' powder (optional)

In a large Dutch oven or soup pot, heat the olive oil over medium heat. Stir in the flour, making your roux. Cook about one minute, until the flour begins to turn a slightly darker brown. Remove from heat. Stir in the onions, celery, garlic, and bell pepper. Return to heat and quickly stir in the chicken broth. Add about 3 cups of water, or enough water to make 6 cups when combined with the broth.

Add the okra, tomatoes and andouille sausage. Stir and bring to a boil, then reduce to a simmer.

Place the lentils in a fine sieve and rinse under cool water. Immediately add the lentils to the pot, breaking the apart with a fork as you add them, if needed. Stir. Simmer 1½ -2 hours.

Just before serving, stir in the Tabasco and gumbo file' powder, if desired. Ladle into bowls and enjoy.

Serves 8.

1 serving: Total Fat (g): 6
             Protein (g): 12
             Total Carbohydrates (g): 21
             Dietary Fiber (g): 10
             197 calories

Food Exchanges: Starch/Bread: 1, Lean Meat: 1, Vegetable: 1½, Fat: 1

*I like to use Aidelles Andouille Sausage for this recipe.

Lentil Chili
Lentils are a nice alternative to traditional kidney beans.

1½ cups lentils
3 cups water or beef broth
1 (14 ½ ounce) can diced tomatoes
2 tablespoons olive oil, divided
½ pound lean ground beef
1 small onion, chopped
3 cloves garlic, crushed
1 ½ teaspoons salt
1 ½ teaspoons ground cumin
2 ½ tablespoons chili powder
1 teaspoon dried oregano
*1 - 2 hot chili peppers, seeded
sour cream, optional
Cheddar cheese, shredded, optional

Rinse the lentils and place in a large saucepan with the water (or broth) and the diced tomatoes. Bring to a simmer.

In a medium pan, sauté the ground beef, onion and garlic in olive oil until translucent. Add to the lentils. Add the salt, cumin, chili powder and oregano.

If you use the hot peppers, slit them and remove the seeds. Remove the stems. Be careful not to touch your face. If your skin is sensitive, use protective gloves! Place the peppers in a processor with about 3 cups of the liquid in which pepper was cooked. Puree. Add to the chili mixture.

Simmer the chili for a total of 2 to 3 hours, the longer, the thicker.

Serve with shredded cheddar and dollop of sour cream.

Serves 6.

1 serving: Total Fat (g): 16
Protein (g): 21
Total Carbohydrates (g): 35
Dietary Fiber (g): 17
337 calories

Food Exchanges: Starch/Bread: 2, Lean Meat: 2, Vegetable: 1, Fat: 2

For False-Alarm Chili, omit hot peppers.

Winter Chili
Nice and warming!

3 tablespoons olive oil
1 pound lean stew beef, diced into ½ inch cubes
1 medium onion, diced
2 cloves garlic, crushed
1 (14.5 ounce) can diced tomatoes
1 (15.5 ounce) can red kidney beans
1 can water
3 tablespoons chili powder
¾ teaspoon ground cumin
1 teaspoon oregano
¼ teaspoon cayenne pepper (optional or to taste)
1 teaspoon salt
1 tablespoon masa or stone ground corn meal

In a large skillet, heat the oil over medium heat.

Sauté the beef, onion and garlic until the onions are translucent and the beef begins to brown.

Add all remaining ingredients except for the masa. Cover and simmer at least 1 hour, up to 2 hours, adding water only if needed.

15 minutes before serving, stir the masa (or corn meal) into 2 tablespoons cold water. Add to the chili. Simmer 15 minutes and serve.

Serves 5.

1 serving: Total Fat (g): 22
Protein (g): 24
Total Carbohydrates (g): 22
Dietary Fiber (g): 8
389 calories

Food Exchanges: Starch/Bread: 1, Lean Meat: 2 ½, Vegetable: 1, Fat: 3

Black Bean Chili
Make it a complete meal with an avocado salad on the side.

1 teaspoon oil
1 pound lean ground beef
1 medium onion, diced
2 cloves garlic, crushed or minced
2 (15 ounce) cans black beans
1 (15 ounce) can diced tomatoes
2 tablespoons chili powder
1/8 teaspoon cayenne pepper (optional)
1 teaspoon salt
1 teaspoon cumin powder
1 teaspoon oregano

Coat the bottom of a large saucepan with oil. Heat, then sauté the beef and onions in the oil until the onions are translucent and the beef is cooked. Stir in the garlic and cook for about one minute. Add the remaining ingredients. Bring to a boil. Simmer 45 minutes or more, stirring occasionally.

Serves 4.

1 serving: Total Fat (g): 27
Protein (g): 32
Total Carbohydrates (g): 38
Dietary Fiber (g): 15
540 calories

Food Exchanges: Starch/Bread: 2, Lean Meat: 4, Vegetable: ½, Fat: 3 ½

Hearty Ham & Black Bean Soup
A perfect comfort food to take off the chill

1 ham bone (optional, but nice)
1 (8 ounce) package dried black beans *
2 cups diced ham
1 tablespoon olive oil
2 ribs celery, diced
½ cup chopped onion
4 ripe tomatoes, seeded and diced (or 1 can diced tomatoes)
1½ teaspoons salt
2 cloves garlic, minced

If you use a ham bone, place it in a large stock pot and cover with water. Bring to a boil, then simmer over low heat for 2-4 hours. The meat should pull away from the bone when ready. Remove from the heat and cool to room temperature. Cover and refrigerate overnight.

The evening before cooking the soup, rinse the black beans. Place them in a large bowl and fill the bowl with water. Cover and allow the beans to soak overnight.

If you use a ham bone: The following morning, remove the ham stock from the refrigerator, pull off the solidified fat from the top and discard. Discard the bone and any fatty parts of the ham, returning the lean ham to the stock. Set the stockpot aside.

Rinse the soaked black beans in a colander. Place them in a large pot of water and bring to a boil. Simmer about an hour. Drain the beans once more, then add them to the ham stock or place them back in the pot with 6 –8 cups of water. Bring to a boil, and then reduce the beans to a simmer.

While the beans are simmering, cut the ham into bite-sized pieces and toss the pieces in with the beans.

In a small skillet, heat the olive oil over medium heat. Add the celery and onion; sauté just until the onions become fragrant and translucent. Add these to the soup, as well. Add the tomatoes, salt and minced garlic. Continue simmering the soup 6 – 8 hours, until the beans become tender. The longer, the better!

Makes 10 hearty servings.

1/10 of recipe, made with dried beans: Total Fat (g): 3
Protein (g): 11
Total Carbohydrates (g): 17
Dietary Fiber (g): 4
154 calories

Food Exchanges: Starch/Bread: 1, Lean Meat: 1, Vegetable: ½, Fat: ½

*Want to skip the long cooking process? Just substitute 3 (14.5 ounce) cans of black beans! Then simmer the ingredients together at least 30 minutes.

Navy Bean Soup

1 cup dried navy beans
1 tablespoon olive oil
½ pound boneless smoked pork chops, cut into cubes
3 stalks celery, cleaned and diced
½ cup onion, chopped
1 teaspoon salt
¼ teaspoon black pepper
2 quarts water

To soak the beans:
Wash the beans, discarding any debris you find. Rinse, then place in a large pot and fill nearly to top with water. Bring the beans to a boil. Remove from heat and cover for 1 hour.

In a skillet, add the olive oil. Over medium heat, add the cubes of pork, celery, and onions. Sauté until the onions are tender and translucent. Remove from the heat.

Drain and rinse the beans*.

Add 2 quarts water to the pot of beans. Bring to a boil. Simmer 3 or more hours, until the beans are tender. The longer it cooks, the thicker the soup.

Serves 4 - 5.

*Never cook beans in the water in which you soak them. Doing so causes most of the gas problems people experience!

1/4 recipe   Total Fat (g): 7
                      Protein (g): 22
                      Total Carbohydrates (g): 34
                      Dietary Fiber (g): 14
                      291 calories

Food Exchanges: Starch/Bread: 2, Lean Meat: 2, Vegetable: ½, Fat: ½

Southwestern Black Bean Soup

8 ounces dried black beans
¼ cup olive oil
1 large onion, chopped
4 cloves garlic, minced
2 jalapeno peppers, minced*
6 cups water
1 (14½ ounce) can diced tomatoes
¼ teaspoon dried mustard
2 teaspoons salt or to taste
3 tablespoons Sherry, optional
salsa and sour cream for garnish (optional)

The evening before, soak the beans according to package directions.

Before cooking, rinse and drain the beans; set aside**.

Heat the oil in a large pot. Add the onions, garlic and peppers. Sauté until the onions are translucent. Add the tomatoes, water, salt and dry mustard. Bring to a boil, and then reduce the heat. Simmer for 3 hours or more, adding water as needed for desired consistency.

Remove about 1/3 of the soup from pot and puree in a blender or food processor. Return to the pot. Add sherry and simmer for 15 minutes.

Garnish with tomato or salsa and a dollop of sour cream.

Makes 8 servings.

1 serving:	
	Total Fat (g): 7
	Protein (g): 7
	Total Carbohydrates (g): 22
	Dietary Fiber (g): 5
	184 calories

Food Exchanges: Starch/Bread: 1½, Lean Meat: ½, Vegetable: 1, Fat: 1½

* *Slit peppers lengthwise and scoop out seeds with spoon, being careful not to touch face with hands. Rinse under cool water. Remove stems. Mince peppers, set aside and wash hands.*

** *Never cook beans in the water in which you soak them. Doing so causes most of the gas problems people experience.*

Tortilla Soup with Chicken

Make this soup extra special by adding a garnish of grated Monterey Jack cheese and a dollop of sour cream. A few slices of avocado on the side make a nice complement to the bit of heat from the poblano.

4 boneless, skinless chicken breasts
½ cup diced onion
1 poblano pepper
1 clove garlic, crushed
2 tablespoons + 1/3 cup olive oil, divided
2 (14.5 ounce) cans chicken broth
1 (14.5 ounce) can diced tomatoes in sauce
¾ teaspoon dried basil
¼ teaspoon black pepper
salt to taste
10 small low carb tortillas (La Tortilla brand)

Dice the onions; set aside. Cut the chicken breasts into ½ inch cubes and set aside.

If you have sensitive skin, wear gloves to prepare the poblano pepper: Cut off the stem, then slice the pepper lengthwise. Using a spoon, scrape out the seeds and discard them. Slice the pepper into thin slices lengthwise, then crosswise to mince it.

In a large pot, heat 2 tablespoons olive oil over medium heat. Add the chicken, onion and pepper; sauté until the onion is translucent and fragrant. Add the garlic and quickly stir in. Stir in the chicken broth, diced tomatoes, basil, pepper, and salt. Bring to a boil, then reduce to a simmer. Continue cooking, uncovered, over very low heat for 30 to 45 minutes.

While the soup is cooking, prepare the tortillas. Slice the tortillas into strips that are about ¼ inch wide. Set aside. In a skillet, heat the 1/3 cup olive oil. Add the tortilla slices, cooking in small amounts, until they are lightly browned, about 30 to45 seconds. Remove each batch and drain on paper towels as you go.

To serve, divide the tortilla strips among the bowls. Ladle the soup over the strips in each bowl. If desired, top each with a sprinkling of Monterey Jack cheese and a dollop of sour cream.

Makes 12 servings.

1 serving: Total Fat (g): 11
              Protein (g): 24
              Total Carbohydrates (g): 13
              Dietary Fiber (g): 8
              239 calories

Food Exchanges: Lean Meat: 2½, Vegetable: ½, Fat: 1½

If you prefer no heat, just substitute a small can of green chiles for the poblano.

Mom's Chicken Soup
The ultimate comfort food for chasing away the chill.

2 chicken breast halves, with skin and bones
¼ cup onion, chopped
¼ cup celery, chopped
1 large clove garlic, minced
1 teaspoon olive oil
1 teaspoon salt
6 cups water
1 cup brown rice (Lundgren's brand has fabulous mixed brown rices)

Place the chicken in a large pot with water. Simmer over very low heat for 1 to 2 hours. Remove the chicken from the broth and allow the chicken to cool. Leave the broth on simmer.

Sauté the onion, celery, and garlic in oil about 3 minutes or until the onion is translucent. Add to the broth. Add the salt.

Remove the skin and bones from the chicken. Chop the chicken into chunky pieces. Add to the pot. Bring to boil. If directed on the package, rinse the rice, then add to the pot.

Reduce heat and simmer for 1 hour or longer. Add water as needed to maintain desired consistency.

Serves 4.

1 serving: Total Fat (g): 9
Protein (g): 19
Total Carbohydrates (g): 38
Dietary Fiber (g): 1
Calories: 313

Food Exchanges: Starch/Bread: 2 ½, Lean Meat: 2, Fat: ½

Chicken and Broccoli Cream Soup

2 tablespoons butter
1 pound boneless, skinless chicken, cut into ½ inch pieces
1 large onion, minced
1 (14.5 ounce) can chicken broth
1½ cups chopped broccoli
4 tablespoons oat bran
¼ teaspoon white pepper
½ teaspoon salt
½ cup heavy cream
¾ cup shredded Swiss cheese

Heat the butter in a large soup pot. Add the chicken pieces and onion and sauté until the onion is translucent. Add the chicken broth, broccoli, oat bran, pepper and salt and simmer over very low heat for 20 minutes. Add the heavy cream and stir. Heat for just another minute or two.

Place about 2 tablespoons Swiss cheese in each individual serving bowl. Ladle the soup into each serving bowl and serve.

Serves 5.

1 serving: Total Fat (g): 20
            Protein (g): 26
            Total Carbohydrates (g): 10
            Dietary Fiber (g): 2
            334 calories

Food Exchanges: Lean Meat: 3, Vegetable: 1, Fat: 3½

French Onion Soup
Serve with a leafy salad for a lovely luncheon!

3 large white onions, thinly sliced
¼ cup butter
2 (14½ ounce) cans beef broth
¼ teaspoon salt
1/8 teaspoon pepper
1 teaspoon Worcestershire sauce
4 slices whole grain bread, cut into cubes and toasted lightly
1 cup Swiss cheese, grated

Sauté the onions in butter until lightly browned.

In a separate pot, combine the broth plus ¼ cup water, Worcestershire sauce, salt and pepper. Cover and cook 30 minutes. May be left to simmer up to 4 hours. Add water as needed as it cooks down.

Serve in ovenproof soup crocks or mugs. Top with toasted, whole grain bread cubes. Sprinkle generously with cheese. Place under the broiler until the cheese is melted and begins to brown. Serve immediately.

Serves 4.

1 serving: Total Fat (g): 22
            Protein (g): 16
            Total Carbohydrates (g): 27
            Dietary Fiber (g): 4
            358 calories

Food Exchanges: Starch/Bread: 1½, Lean Meat: 1, Vegetable: 1, Fat: 3½

Butternut Squash Soup
A warm winter supper. Serve with a slice of apple bread.

2 cups chicken broth
1 butternut squash, cooked and cooled
2 medium onions, diced
1 tablespoon butter or oil
1 cup sour cream
1 cup half & half
1½ teaspoon salt
½ teaspoons ground white pepper

Pour the chicken broth into a large saucepan or soup pot.

After the squash is cooled, scoop out the flesh and add to the chicken broth. Bring to a boil and simmer for 10 minutes.

Meanwhile, sauté the onions in oil until translucent and tender. Add to the squash mixture. Let cool 10 minutes.

Pour half of the squash mixture into a processor and process until smooth. Transfer to a separate container. Repeat with the remaining mixture.

Return the squash mixture to the saucepan. Stir in the remaining ingredients. Cook over low heat, stirring constantly, just until heated _or_ chill 2 hours. Serve hot or cold.

Serves 6.

1 serving: Total Fat (g): 15
Protein (g): 7
Total Carbohydrates (g): 40
Dietary Fiber (g): 5
307 calories

Food Exchanges: Starch/Bread: 2, Vegetable: ½, Non-fat milk: ½, Fat: 3

Curried Mushroom Bisque
Fenugreek seeds, found in curry, have been used for centuries to treat diabetes; these seeds are believed to help control blood sugar. Try this scrumptiously spicy soup; quick and easy to make.

2 cups diced onions
2 tablespoons butter
2 cloves garlic, crushed
½ cup water
2 (14.4 oz) cans chicken broth
¼ teaspoons ground ginger
4 teaspoons curry powder
2 tablespoons oat bran
1 cup sliced wild or mixed mushrooms
½ cup heavy cream
Salt and pepper to taste

In a large saucepan, melt the butter and add the onions. Sauté until the onions become translucent. Add the crushed garlic and stir. Add the water, broth, ginger, curry and oat bran. Cover and simmer for 15 minutes.

Add all mushrooms, except for 8 slices. Puree the soup with a hand blender or place in processor to puree. Return the soup to low heat. Add heavy cream and mix in. Do not boil. Salt and pepper to taste.

Serve in soup bowls, placing 2 of the reserved mushroom slices in each bowl.

Makes 4 servings.

1 serving: Total Fat (g): 15
              Protein (g): 7
              Total Carbohydrates (g): 13
              Dietary Fiber (g): 3

Food Exchanges: Lean Meat: ½, Vegetables: 1½, Fat: 2½

Creamy Tomato Soup

Try this tasty tomato soup hot or chilled. It's delicious either way!

2 tablespoons olive oil
½ cup finely minced onion
1 clove garlic, crushed
1/8 teaspoon ground cinnamon
1 (28 ounce) can crushed tomatoes
1 cup water
¼ teaspoon ground cumin
½ teaspoon ground coriander
½ teaspoon salt
1 tablespoon lime juice or lemon juice
½ cup heavy cream

In a heavy saucepan, sauté the onions in the olive oil until the onions become translucent. Stir in the garlic.

Add all the remaining ingredients except for the heavy cream. Bring to a boil. Immediately reduce the heat and simmer for 10 minutes.

Remove from the heat and stir in the cream. If you prefer a smoother consistency, puree in a blender.

Serve hot or let cool and refrigerate.

Makes 5 (1 cup) servings.

1 serving: Total Fat (g): 15
               Protein (g): 3
               Total Carbohydrates (g): 14
               Dietary Fiber (g): 3
               189 calories

Food Exchanges: Vegetable: 2½, Fat: 3

Curried Sweet Potato Soup
Delicious chilled or served piping hot!

2 (14 ½ ounce) cans chicken broth
1 medium onion, minced
2 tablespoons olive oil
2 large sweet potatoes, baked and peeled
2 cups heavy cream
1 ½ teaspoons curry powder
¼ teaspoon salt
1/8 teaspoon black pepper
grated zest* of one lemon
3 tablespoons sherry

In a large saucepan, bring the chicken broth to boil, and then reduce to simmer.

In a small saucepan, sauté the onion in the oil until the onion is tender and just begins to brown. Add the onions to the chicken broth.

In a processor, puree the sweet potatoes with heavy cream. Add the sweet potatoes to the chicken broth with a wire whip, mixing until smooth. Add the curry, salt, pepper, lemon zest and sherry. Remove from heat.

May be eaten hot or chilled.

Serves 6 to 8.

1/6 recipe: Total Fat (g): 35
Protein (g): 6
Total Carbohydrates (g): 16
Dietary Fiber (g): 2
403 calories

Food Exchanges: Starch/Bread: ½, Lean Meat: 1, Vegetable: ½, Fat: 7

Lemon zest is the colored part of the lemon peel.

Roasted Squash & Apple Soup
Roast the squash the night before; then whip together this tasty soup the next day.

½ spaghetti squash
1 medium acorn squash
2 (14 ½ ounce) cans chicken broth
½ cup diced onions
1 tablespoon butter
1 tablespoon freshly grated ginger root
1 teaspoon curry powder
2 Granny Smith apples
1 teaspoon salt
2 tablespoons sherry
dash cayenne, to taste
½ cup heavy cream

To roast the squash: Preheat the oven to 400 degrees.
Cut each squash in half lengthwise. With a large spoon, scoop out the seeds and strings. Since the spaghetti squash requires more cooking time than the acorn squash, place the spaghetti squash flesh-side-down on a baking sheet. Place it in the oven. After 15 minutes, place both halves of the acorn squash (flesh-side-down) on the baking sheet with the spaghetti squash. Continue baking for an additional 45 minutes. When done, the squash should feel soft to the touch. Remove from the oven. Cool slightly.

Using a large spoon, scoop out the acorn squash and the spaghetti squash half; then place the squash scoopings in a large bowl until ready to use for the soup. If you roast both halves of the spaghetti squash, scoop the "meat" from one of the halves with a fork and place in a separate bowl to use in a different dish. It can be used hot or cold like pasta.

To make the soup: Place the squash in a food processor. Add one can of chicken broth. Puree. Leave the mixture in the processor.

Melt the butter in a large Dutch oven or soup pot. Stir in the onions, apples, ginger root, and curry powder. Sauté until onions and apples are soft. Add this mixture to the food processor. Puree all together.

Return the squash mixture to the Dutch oven or soup pot. Add the additional can of chicken broth and about 1½ cups water, to desired consistency. Add the salt, sherry, and cayenne. Bring to a boil and simmer 10 minutes. Remove from heat; stir in the heavy cream. Nice served with a dollop of unsweetened whipped cream on each bowl.

8 servings.

1 serving:	Total Fat (g): 8	*Food Exchanges:*
	Protein (g): 3	Starch/Bread 1½, Vegetable: ½,
	Total Carbohydrates (g): 12	Fruit: ½, Fat: 1½
	Dietary Fiber (g): 2	
	130 calories	

Cream of Broccoli Soup
Quick to make, and broccoli is a wonderful way to control blood sugar.

1 pound fresh or frozen broccoli, chopped
2 (14 ½ ounce) cans chicken broth
¼ cup butter
¼ cup whole-wheat flour
½ cup half & half
dash cayenne pepper
½ teaspoon salt

Place the broccoli on a microwave safe dish. Loosely cover with plastic wrap and microwave on high for 2 minutes. Set aside.

Melt the butter in a large pot. Remove it from the heat and stir in the flour. Gradually add the broth, stirring with whisk.

Return to the heat, cooking over medium heat. Stir constantly, until slightly thickened. Reduce the temperature to simmer. Stir in half & half, pepper, salt and broccoli. Heat through.

Serves 6.

1 serving:
Total Fat (g): 11
Protein (g): 5
Total Carbohydrates (g): 7
Dietary Fiber (g): 2
154 calories

Food Exchanges: Lean Meat: ½, Vegetable: 1, Fat: 2

Broccoli-Cheddar Soup:
Add 1 cup sharp, shredded cheddar, along with final ingredients.

Serves 6.

1 serving:
Total Fat (g): 17
Protein (g): 10
Total Carbohydrates (g): 8
Dietary Fiber (g): 2
230 calories

Food Exchanges: Lean Meat: 1, Vegetable: ½, Fat: 3

Beefy Rice & Mushroom Soup

3 tablespoons olive oil
½ pounds lean beef, cut into ½ inch cubes
1 medium onion, chopped
2 (10 ½ ounce) cans double strength beef broth
¼ teaspoon thyme
¼ teaspoon black pepper
2 cups water
½ cup wild rice
½ pound mushrooms, sliced

In large saucepan, heat oil. Sauté the beef and onions until the beef begins to brown. Add broth, water pepper and thyme. Simmer 1 - 4 hours. The longer it simmers, the more tender the beef. Add water as needed.

One hour before serving, add the rice and additional water if necessary. Continue to simmer.

About 5 minutes before serving, add the mushrooms and simmer 5 minutes.

Serves 4.

1 serving: Total Fat (g): 22
Protein (g): 21
Total Carbohydrates (g): 22
Dietary Fiber (g): 2
342 calories

Food Exchanges: Starch/Bread: 1, Lean Meat: 2, Vegetable: 1, Fat: 3

Santa Fe Soup

Easy to make and a nice change of pace. Serve with salad and corn sticks.

1 medium onion, chopped in 1 inch pieces
3 small jalapeno or serrano chiles, seeded (use gloves and do not touch face)
3 tablespoons butter
1 (10½ ounces) can chicken broth plus 1 can of water
¼ cup dry white wine or water
6 tablespoons whole wheat flour*
2 cups half & half
1½ cups sharp cheddar cheese, shredded
1½ cups Colby/Jack cheese, shredded
1/8 teaspoons black pepper
½ teaspoons salt
½ cup fresh cilantro, minced
1 (14½ ounce) can diced tomatoes, drained

Process the onion and chilies until finely minced.

Melt the butter. Add the onions and chilies and cook until softened and the onions just begin to brown, about 5 minutes. Add the stock and wine; bring to a boil. Reduce heat and simmer 30 minutes.

Measure the flour into a large bowl. Gradually whisk in the half & half. Stir into the saucepan with the stock. Cook over medium heat until slightly thickened, stirring constantly, about 2 minutes. Stir in the cheeses. Cook over low heat until smooth, stirring frequently. Season with salt and pepper.

Mix cilantro and drained tomatoes in small bowl. Ladle the soup into bowls; drop a spoonful of the tomato mixture into the middle of each.

*Kamut or spelt flour may be substituted.

Serves 6.

1 serving: Total Fat (g): 34
               Protein (g): 19
               Total Carbohydrates (g): 15
               Dietary Fiber (g): 2

Food Exchanges: Starch/Bread: ½, Lean Meat: 2, Vegetable: 1, Non-fat milk: ½, Fat: 5½,

Seafood

Cajun Catfish
A down home Sunday supper.

1½ pounds catfish filets
1 egg, mixed with 1 tablespoon water
½ cup stone ground cornmeal
½ teaspoon salt
1 teaspoon Old Bay Seasoning
½ teaspoon cayenne pepper
¼ cup olive oil

Rinse the catfish under cool water, drain on paper towels, then place in a bowl with the egg mixture. Toss to coat the fish with egg.

Mix the cornmeal, salt, seasoning, and pepper in a shallow dish or plate.

Add about ¼ inch of oil to the skillet. Heat over medium-high heat until a drop of water sizzles when added.

Dredge the catfish in the cornmeal mixture and fry 3 - 4 minutes, turning only once, until the fish is browned and cooked through. Drain on paper towels. Repeat until all fish is cooked, adding additional oil as needed. Serve hot.

Serves 4.

1 serving: Total Fat (g): 20
Protein (g): 30
Total Carbohydrates (g): 12
Dietary Fiber (g): 12
354 calories

Food Exchanges: Starch/Bread: 1, Lean Meat: 4, Fat: 3

Salmon with Cucumber Sauce
Elegant, simple and lovely for guests.

6 fresh salmon filets (about 6 ounces each)
1 tablespoon olive oil
1 tablespoon lemon juice

Cucumber Sauce
1 small cucumber, peeled, seeded, and diced
1 cup sour cream
1 tablespoon sugar-free mayonnaise
1 teaspoon lemon juice
¼ cup fresh dill, chopped (or 1 tablespoon dried dill)
¼ teaspoon dried mustard
¼ teaspoon salt

Place all the Cucumber Sauce ingredients in a blender or food processor. Process until the mixture is smooth and there are small chunks of cucumber. Refrigerate until ready to serve.

Rinse the salmon with cool water. Pat dry with paper towels.

Heat the grill or broiler.

Mix the olive oil and lemon juice. Brush the salmon with the oil and lemon mixture. Broil the fish, turning once, just until the fish flakes all the way through when fork is inserted and twisted (about 15 minutes). Serve with the sauce on the side.

Serves 6.

Makes 12 cups.

1/6 recipe Total Fat (g): 18
Protein (g): 36
Total Carbohydrates (g): 3
Dietary Fiber (g): trace
323 calories

Food Exchanges: Lean Meat: 5, Vegetable: ½, Fat: 2½

Grilled Salmon with Lemon Dill Sauce

Delicious year-round, salmon is a fabulous source of Omega-3's. Adding Omega-3's regularly to the diet can help reverse insulin resistance. Try this delightful dish for a great addition to your menu.

1 tablespoon olive oil
1 tablespoon lemon juice
4 salmon filets, about 6 ounce each

Lemon Dill Sauce

1 tablespoon stoneground mustard
1 teaspoon dry mustard
3 teaspoons chopped fresh dill (or 1 teaspoon dried dill)
¼ cup mayonnaise (sugar free, if possible)
2 tablespoons lemon juice

Combine olive oil and 1 tablespoon lemon juice in small container and set aside.

Rinse salmon with cool water. Pat dry with paper towels. Brush with lemon-olive oil mixture and grill or broil to desired doneness. Be sure to place flesh-side toward the heat, skin-side away from heat to prevent curling. Turn after about 7 minutes and cook to desired doneness.

While the salmon cooks, prepare the lemon dill sauce by combining the remaining ingredients in a small bowl.

Remove the salmon to platter and serve with the sauce on the side.

Serves 4.

1 serving: Total Fat (g): 20 (before cooking)
          Protein (g): 34
          Total Carbohydrates (g): 1
          Dietary Fiber (g): 0
          336 calories

Food Exchanges: Lean Meat: 5, Fat: 1½, Other Carb: ½

BBQ Party Shrimp
This recipe is always a crowd pleaser!

½ cup butter
2 cups celery, finely minced
3 cloves garlic, crushed
2 cups BBQ sauce (see table of contents)
1 cup lemon juice
4 dozen jumbo shrimp, cleaned and deveined
lettuce leaves

Melt the butter in a skillet. Add the celery. Sauté until softened, then stir in the garlic.

Add the BBQ sauce and lemon juice. Simmer for 20 minutes, uncovered, over low heat. Stir as needed.

Add the shrimp and simmer just until the shrimp is cooked through, about 5 minutes.

Arrange the lettuce leaveson a platter. Place the shrimp on the lettuce and serve with a side of sauce.

Serves 8.

1 serving Total Fat (g): 15
Protein (g): 10
Total Carbohydrates (g): 15
Dietary Fiber (g): 3
225 calories

Food Exchanges: Lean Meat: 1, Vegetable: ½, Fat: 2 ½

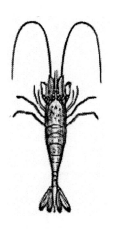

Shrimp Creole
Straight from the Bayou! Serve with salad and whole grain bread.

3 tablespoons olive oil
½ cup onion, chopped
½ cup celery, chopped
3 cloves garlic, minced
1 (1 lb.) can diced tomatoes
1 (12 ounce) can tomato puree
1 teaspoon salt
2 teaspoons chili powder
dash cayenne pepper, to taste (optional)
1 tablespoon Worcestershire sauce
1/8 teaspoon Tabasco
1 pound cleaned, de-veined raw shrimp
3 tablespoons green pepper

Heat the oil in a skillet over medium heat. Add the onion and the celery. Stir until the onion is translucent. Add the garlic and stir about 1 minute. Add the tomatoes, tomato puree, salt, cayenne, chili powder, Worcestershire sauce and Tabasco. Simmer 30 minutes.

Add the shrimp and green pepper. Simmer until the shrimp are cooked through, about 5 minutes.

Serve over brown or wild rice.

Serves 6.

1 serving (w/out rice): Total Fat (g): 9
Protein (g): 17
Total Carbohydrates (g): 13
Dietary Fiber (g): 3
193 calories

Food Exchanges: Lean Meat: 2, Vegetable: 2, Fat: 1½

Peppered Swordfish
Sea bass may be substituted.

6 swordfish steaks (about 6 ounces each)
½ cup dry white wine
¼ cup lemon juice
1 teaspoon soy sauce
½ teaspoon Worcestershire sauce
1 clove garlic

1 tablespoon coarsely ground pepper
1/8 teaspoon ground cayenne pepper

Blend all ingredients except the fish.

Rinse the fish under cool water and pat dry. Dip the fish in marinade, turning once. Grill about 12 minutes per side or just until the fish flakes when a fork is inserted in center.

Marinade makes about ¾ cup.

Serves 6.

1 serving: Total Fat (g): 7
          Protein (g): 34
          Total Carbohydrates (g): 1
          Dietary Fiber (g): trace
          227 calories

Food Exchanges: Lean Meat: 4½, Fat: 1½

Virginia Crab Cakes
Make ahead; then, refrigerate until ready to cook.

1 pound lump crabmeat
3 tablespoons oat bran
1/3 cup half & half
2 eggs
1 teaspoon dried mustard
½ teaspoon salt
1/8 teaspoon pepper
1 teaspoon sugar-free mayonnaise
3 slices whole grain bread (about 2 cups soft bread crumbs)
1 teaspoon paprika
½ olive oil

Rinse the crabmeat with cold water. Drain thoroughly and remove any pieces of shell that may remain. Refrigerate.

In a small bowl, mix the oat bran, half & half, eggs, mustard, salt, pepper, and mayonnaise. Set aside.

Tear the bread into large pieces. Place in a processor and process into fine crumbs. Mix ¼ cup breadcrumbs into the egg mixture. Place the remaining crumbs in a shallow dish.

Gently mix the egg mixture with the crabmeat. Cook immediately as directed below or cover and refrigerate for use later in the day.

To cook: Heat the oil in a skillet on medium-high. Form the crabmeat into 8 patties, each about ½ inch thick. Dip both sides of each into remaining the breadcrumbs. Cook in hot oil, turning once. Drain on paper towels.

Serves 8.

1 serving   Total Fat (g): 11*
              Protein (g): 15
              Total Carbohydrates (g): 9
              Dietary Fiber (g): 1
              188 calories

Food Exchanges: Starch/Bread: ½, Lean Meat: 2, Fat: 2*

*Counts assume half the oil remains. Actual fat count is probably less, depending on how well drained.

Cucumber Sauce (see table of contents) makes a nice accompaniment.

Crab Mornay

This is an especially nice dish for a buffet or a dinner party. Prepare it ahead of time, and then pop it in the oven just before your guests arrive. If you refrigerate this ahead of time, be sure to allow a few extra minutes for cooking.

4 tablespoons butter, melted
1 small onion, grated
4 tablespoons whole wheat flour
1 (14.5 ounce) can chicken broth
½ teaspoon salt
¾ cup heavy cream
1 pound lump crabmeat
2 eggs
2 tablespoons grated parmesan cheese

Preheat the oven to 350 degrees. Grease or spray a 1½-quart casserole or 4 individual casseroles.

Mornay Sauce

In a medium saucepan, melt butter over medium heat. Add onion and stir to heat, but do not brown. With a whisk, quickly stir in flour, then chicken broth, salt and 2 tablespoons heavy cream. Bring to a boil, stirring constantly. Lower the heat to a simmer and cook 3 - 5 additional minutes, stirring to keep the bottom of the sauce from browning or lumping. Remove from the heat.

Place the crabmeat in a colander and rinse under cold water. Drain thoroughly, then pat dry with a paper towel to remove the excess moisture.

In a large mixing bowl, beat the eggs with ½ cup of the heavy cream. Add all but 2 tablespoons sauce to the egg mixture and thoroughly combine. With a large spoon, gently mix in the crabmeat, preserving the lumps as much as possible. Spoon the mixture into the casserole dish.

To the 2 tablespoons of reserved sauce, add the Parmesan cheese and the remaining 2 tablespoons of heavy cream. Spread gently over the top of the casserole.

Bake about 45 minutes, until hot and bubble, with the top nicely browned.

Serves 4.

1 serving: Total Fat (g): 33
                Protein (g): 29
                Total Carbohydrates (g): 10
                Dietary Fiber (g): 1
                451 calories

Food Exchanges: Starch/Bread: ½, Lean Meat: 3½, Fat: 6, Vegetable: ½

Oyster Casserole with Artichoke Hearts
A taste of New Orleans

¼ cup oat bran
3 tablespoons butter, divided
2 ½ tablespoons whole-wheat flour
1 large, sweet onion, diced (about 2 cups)
1 (16 ounce) container fresh shucked oysters with juices (about 16 oysters)
1 (14 ounce) can artichoke hearts, rinsed, drained, and lightly mashed
¼ teaspoon thyme
¼ teaspoon salt
black pepper to taste
1 slice whole grain bread, torn into small pieces
¼ cup Parmesan cheese

Preheat oven to 350 degrees.

Lightly butter or grease a 2-quart casserole dish. Sprinkle the bottom of the dish evenly with oat bran. Set aside.

In a large skillet, melt 1-tablespoon butter. Sauté the onion over medium-high until tender and translucent. Remove to a small dish and set aside.

Place the skillet over heat once again. Melt the remaining 2 tablespoons butter. Stir in flour and spices, then cook over medium high heat until the mixture bubbles and the flour begins to slightly darken. Remove the flour mixture to a small dish and set aside.

Reduce the heat to medium-low. Pour the oysters with juices into the skillet. Simmer 3 - 4 minutes, until the edges begin to curl, turning the oysters once. With a slotted spoon, remove the oysters to the casserole, placing them in an even layer over the oat bran.

With a whisk, stir the roux (flour mixture) into the remaining liquid. Add the mashed artichoke hearts with the onions, thyme, salt and pepper. Spoon evenly over the top of the oysters.

Combine the soft breadcrumbs and Parmesan cheese in a small bowl. Sprinkle evenly over the top of the casserole.

Bake in for about 15 minutes, until the breadcrumbs are golden brown.

Serves 4.

1 serving: Total Fat (g): 14
              Protein (g): 17
              Total Carbohydrates (g): 30
              Dietary Fiber (g): 8
              293 calories

Food Exchanges: Starch/Bread: 1, Lean Meat: 1½, Vegetable: 2½, Fat: 2

Flounder with Saffron Sauce

½ teaspoon saffron threads, loosely measured
½ tablespoon boiling water
2 tablespoons plain yogurt
¼ cup sour cream
1/8 teaspoon salt
1 small clove garlic, crushed
1½ pounds flounder filets
½ cup whole wheat flour
olive oil

To make the saffron sauce:

Place the saffron threads in a small container and cover with boiling water. Cover and let steep for at least 15 minutes.

Combine the yogurt, sour cream, salt, and garlic. With a fork, whisk in the saffron water. Refrigerate until ready to serve.

To cook the fish:

Rinse the fish under cool water and pat dry on paper towels.

Heat the oil on medium-high. Dredge the fish in the whole-wheat flour. Cook the fish in hot oil, skin side up, for 2 - 3 minutes. Turn the fish over and continue cooking for several more minutes or until the fish flakes in the thickest part when a fork is inserted. Remove and drain on paper towels. Place on a platter and serve with saffron sauce.

Serves 4.

1 serving Total Fat (g): 12
Protein (g): 35
Total Carbohydrates (g): 12
Dietary Fiber (g): 2
302 calories

Food Exchanges: Starch/Bread: ½, Lean Meat: 4½, Fat: ½

When cooking fish with skin, always cook with the skin side up first, then turn the fish over. Doing so prevents the fish from curling during the cooking process.

Trout Meuniere
So tasty!

¾ cup unsalted butter
1 teaspoon black pepper
4 tablespoons lemon juice
4 (6 - 8 ounce) fresh trout filets
½ cup whole-wheat flour
½ teaspoon salt
pinch each: black pepper and cayenne pepper
olive oil
parsley and lemon wedges for garnish (optional)

To make the meuniere sauce:
Melt the butter over low heat until slightly browned. Add the pepper and lemon juice, remove from heat and set aside.

Add enough oil to cover the bottom of a large skillet about 1/8 inch deep. Heat over medium heat.

To cook the trout:
Dredge the trout filets in flour. Over medium heat, sauté trout, 2 at a time, cooking skin-side-up first. When browned, turn over and cook several minutes more. Do not allow the oil to over-heat to the point of smoking.

Serve immediately, topped with meuniere sauce. Garnish with lemon wedges and parsley, if desired.

Serves 4.

1 serving: Total Fat (g): 53
Protein (g): 38
Total Carbohydrates (g): 7
Dietary Fiber (g): 2
647 calories

Food Exchanges: Starch/Bread: ½, Lean Meat: 5, Fat: 8½

Sesame Grilled Tuna

Rich in omega-3's, tuna is an easy fish to prepare. Just don't overcook!

4 (1/3 lb. each) tuna filets
2 teaspoons sesame seeds
3 teaspoons dry mustard
1 teaspoon toasted sesame oil
¼ cup olive oil
¼ teaspoon cayenne pepper
1 teaspoon salt

Heat the grill.

Rinse tuna filets under cold water; pat dry with paper towels.

Place the sesame seeds in a small hot skillet for about 1 minute, shaking the skillet gently, until just browned. Remove immediately from heat. Place in a small bowl.

Add the remaining ingredients to the bowl with the toasted seeds. Brush this mixture onto both sides of tuna filets and grill to desired doneness*, turning once.

Serves 4.

1 serving: Total Fat (g): 18
                 Protein (g): 36
                 Total Carbohydrates (g): trace
                 Dietary Fiber: trace

Food Exchanges: Lean Meat: 4½, Fat: 3

* Remove the tuna <u>before</u> it is to the desired doneness. It will continue to cook and will be dry if overcooked. For tuna at its tastiest, take up when rare or pink.

Meat

Stuffed Pork Tenderloin
Always a hit and fun to make!

1 (1 pound) pork tenderloin
1 teaspoon olive oil
¼ cup onion, diced
¼ cup chopped almonds
1 tablespoon sugar-free apricot jam
2 teaspoons oat bran

Preheat the oven to 350 degrees. Prepare a rectangular casserole by spraying with a non-stick spray or coat with oil.

Remove excess fat from the tenderloin. Split lengthwise once; open. Split lengthwise twice more, this time making each slit through the thickest part between the center and the outer edge. Do not cut all the way through! The meat should be fairly flat after the three slits are made. Place in the greased casserole.

In a small skillet, heat the oil. Add the onions and cook until the onions begin to brown. Add the almonds and continue to cook until the onion deepens in color. Stir in the jam until the jam melts and is evenly mixed. Add the oat bran and mix well.

Spread the onion mixture on the pork tenderloin. Bring the edges of the pork together, leaving slightly open at the top so that the mixture shows along the length of the tenderloin. Tie with string in several places, so that the tenderloin holds together (unflavored dental floss works well).

Bake for about 40 minutes or until a meat thermometer inserted in center registers 170 degrees.

Slice crosswise and arrange on small platter.

Serves 4.

1 serving: Total Fat (g): 10
Protein (g): 26
Total Carbohydrates (g): 5
Dietary Fiber (g): 1
214 calories

Food Exchanges: Lean Meat: 3½, Fat: 1

Pork Tenderloin with Lime Soaked Apples

Pork tenderloin medallions with low glycemic apples, what could be tastier? All you need is a nice leafy salad or green vegetable on the side.

2 pork tenderloins (about 1½ pounds – one package usually has 2 tenderloins)
3 medium apples, about 3 cups when sliced
juice of 1 lime (about 3 tablespoons)
2 spring onions, sliced
1/8 teaspoon cinnamon
1/8 teaspoon dried basil
5 tablespoons butter (not margarine), divided

The pork tenderloin is more easily sliced when slightly frozen. Rinse each pork tenderloin under cold water and pat dry. Remove excess fat and the long tendon with a sharp knife by running the knife underneath the tendon. Slice the tenderloins into ¾ inch medallions. Lay on paper towels to finish thawing while you prepare the apples.

Peel, core, and slice the apples into ¼ inch slices. Add the sliced spring onions, cinnamon and basil. Pour the lime juice over the apples and onions; then, mix to coat the apples with the lime juice, combining all. Set aside to marinate.

Heat the oven to 325 degrees. Prepare a baking dish by spraying or buttering lightly.

In a large skillet, heat 3 tablespoons butter over medium heat until melted. Add the pork medallions and sear, cooking on both sides until nearly cooked, about 5 – 8 minutes. Remove from heat and place the medallions in the baking dish; place in the preheated oven.

Return the skillet to medium heat and add the remaining 2 tablespoons of butter. Melt the butter and add the apple mixture. Cook, stirring occasionally to desired doneness, about 10 to 15 minutes. Remove from heat.

Remove the pork medallions from the oven, checking to be sure they are cooked through. Place on a serving platter. Spoon the apple mixture over the tenderloins and serve.

Serves 4 to 5.

¼ recipe: Total Fat (g): 21
Protein (g): 38
Total Carbohydrates (g): 14
Dietary Fiber (g): 2
398 calories

Food Exchanges: Lean Meat: 5½, Fruit: 1, Fat: 3

Mandarin Pork
It tastes as nice as it looks!

1 pound boneless pork loin, cut into ½ inch cubes
2 tablespoons whole grain flour
2 tablespoons sesame oil
1 green pepper, seeded and cut into thin strips
1 medium onion, sliced
1 small can pineapple chunks in it's own juice (no added sugar)
¼ cup soy sauce
¼ cup sherry
2 teaspoons fructose
1 teaspoon freshly grated ginger
½ cup snow peas, fresh or frozen

Dredge the pork cubes in flour. Heat the oil in a large skillet or wok. Add the pork, stirring as needed until browned on all sides.

Drain the pineapple, reserving the liquid, and set aside.

Add the peppers, pineapple, and onions to the pork, stirring until onions are crisp-tender.

Add the pineapple juice, soy sauce, sherry, fructose, ginger, and snow peas. Heat on low for 3 minutes. Add the snow peas. Cook an additional 3 minutes and serve.

Makes 5 servings.

1 serving: Total Fat (g): 10
          Protein (g): 18
          Total Carbohydrates (g): 15
          Dietary Fiber (g): 2
          230 calories

Food Exchanges: Lean Meat: 2½, Vegetable: 1

Pork Fried Rice
Cook the rice ahead of time for a hurry-up meal.

2 cups cooked brown rice (long cooking)
2 cooked pork chops, cut into cubes*
2 tablespoons soy sauce
2 teaspoons water
2 teaspoons sherry
2 tablespoons sesame oil, divided
1 egg, beaten with 1 teaspoon water
2 green onions with tops, sliced
¼ cup green peas
½ teaspoon ginger, freshly grated

Combine the soy sauce, water, and sherry. Add the pork and cover.

Heat 1 tablespoon oil in skillet. Add the eggs and scramble until firm. Remove and chop into small pieces, as desired. Set aside.

Add 1 tablespoon oil to the skillet and heat. Remove the pork from the marinade and add to the skillet. Add the onions and ginger to the pork and cook until heated through. Add the rice and stir to coat. Add the marinade and eggs and heat through.

Serves 4.

1 serving: Total Fat (g): 20
Protein (g): 22
Total Carbohydrates (g): 26
Dietary Fiber (g): 2
400 calories

Food Exchanges: Starch/Bread: 1½, Lean Meat: 2½, Vegetable: ½, Fat: 2

*Leftover shrimp or chicken can be substituted.

Roasted Pork Loin with Sweet Potatoes
A delicious family meal.

1 (2 ½ pound) pork loin roast
2 tablespoons olive oil, divided
1 teaspoon thyme
1 teaspoon marjoram
¼ teaspoon black pepper
½ teaspoon salt
3 large sweet potatoes

Preheat the oven to 450 degrees.

Mix 1 tablespoon olive oil, thyme, marjoram, pepper, and salt. Rub this into the surface of roast. Place the roast in the preheated oven for 15 minutes, uncovered.

Peel the sweet potatoes. Cut crosswise into 2-inch chunks. Brush with the remaining 1 tablespoon of olive oil.

Place in the roasting pan with the pork roast. Tent loosely with aluminum foil. Reduce the oven temperature to 325 degrees. Roast for 2 hours or until a meat thermometer inserted in the center of the meat registers 170 degrees internal temperature.

Serves 6.

1 serving: Total Fat (g): 13
             Protein (g): 35
             Total Carbohydrates (g): 16
             Dietary Fiber (g): 2
             328 calories

Food Exchanges: Starch/Bread: 1, Lean Meat: 2½, Fat: 1

Pork Tenderloin with Lemon Cream Sauce
One of our favorites!

1 lemon
½ cup whole-wheat flour
½ teaspoon salt
2 pork tenderloins (one package usually has two tenderloins), about 1½ pounds
½ cup butter
¾ cup heavy cream

Grate the zest of the lemon (yellow part only) into a small bowl. Squeeze the juice into the zest and set aside.

Combine the flour with the salt and set aside.

Slice each tenderloin lengthwise, but not all the way through. Make another lengthwise slit between the center and the edge of the meat, again being careful not to slice all the way through. Place the meat onto plastic wrap. Place another piece of plastic over. Pound <u>lightly</u> with the flat side of a meat mallet until the thickness is fairly even throughout. Cut each tenderloin in half, so that there are 4 portions.

Melt the butter in a skillet over medium heat. Dredge each tenderloin in the flour mixture and place in a hot skillet. Reduce the heat to medium-low and cook about 8 minutes per side, until just done. Remove the skillet from the heat and place the meat on a platter. Drain the excess butter from pan and discard.

Return the skillet to the stove over low heat. Add the cream; stir in the lemon juice and zest. Keep over the lowest possible heat until the sauce is warm - do not boil. Pour over the tenderloin and serve.

Serves 4.

1 serving: Total Fat (g): 45*
                 Protein (g): 37
                 Total Carbohydrates (g): 2
                 Dietary Fiber (g): trace
                 587 calories

Food Exchanges: Lean Meat: 5, Fat: 8*

*Includes all fat from recipe.

Apricot Glazed Baby Backs

Crispy in the oven or great on the grill, these ribs are delicious! The sweetness comes from low-glycemic apricots and a touch of stevia.

2 slabs baby back ribs, about 2 pounds
¼ cup olive oil
½ cup red wine vinegar
1 teaspoon soy sauce
1 teaspoon sherry
¼ cup water
¾ cups dried apricots, chopped or sliced
¼ teaspoon cayenne pepper
2 small packets powdered stevia (or 2 teaspoons Splenda)

About 3 hours before serving, place the ribs, covered, in a large baking dish or pan. Place in a 325 degree oven and bake.

To make the sauce, place all the remaining ingredients in a blender or a food processor. Puree the sauce until it is fairly smooth.

If baking the ribs:

One hour before serving (after 2 hours of baking time) brush the apricot sauce onto the ribs. Continue baking, uncovered, for at least another hour.

If grilling the ribs:

Place the ribs on the grill at this time and cook on low or indirect heat for another 30 minutes. Then, brush the ribs with the apricot sauce and cook for the remaining 30 minutes.

Remove from heat and cut the ribs into smaller portions, with about 3 ribs each.

If desired, heat the remaining apricot sauce in the microwave and serve as a condiment.

Serves 5.

1 serving: Total Fat (g): 64 (before cooking)
           Protein (g): 37
           Total Carbohydrates (g): 14
           Dietary Fiber (g): 2
           465 calories (before cooking)

Food Exchanges: Lean Meat: 5, Fruit: 1, Fat: 10½ (before cooking)

Veal Parmesan

4 veal cutlets, cubed or pounded flat (about 1½ pounds)
1 egg, beaten with 1 tablespoon water
½ cup dried whole grain breadcrumbs (see index)
¼ cup onion, diced
2 cloves garlic, thinly sliced
1 (14½ ounce) can diced tomatoes
1 (10¾ ounce) can tomato puree
½ cup fresh basil (or 1 tablespoon dried basil)
½ teaspoon salt
olive oil
1 cup mozzarella cheese, shredded

Grease a 2-quart casserole dish and set aside. Preheat the oven to 350 degrees.

Heat a small amount of oil, enough to coat the bottom, in a large skillet. Dip the veal into the egg mixture, then into the breadcrumbs to coat. Add to the skillet and sear on each side, turning once. They do not need to be cooked through. Arrange the cutlets in the casserole dish and set aside.

Quickly add the onion to the skillet. Stir over medium heat until the onion is translucent. Add the garlic and stir over heat about 1 minute. Add the tomatoes, puree, basil and salt. Pour the tomato mixture over the cutlets in the casserole dish. Top with the shredded mozzarella cheese.

Bake 30 minutes at 350 degrees, until the cheese melts and begins to brown.

Serves 4.

1 serving: Total Fat (g): 24
             Protein (g): 43
             Total Carbohydrates (g): 19
             Dietary Fiber (g): 4
             467 calories

Food Exchanges: Lean Meat: 5½, Vegetable: 2½, Fat: 2

Serve with a low glycemic or low carb pasta. Low glycemic pastas include those that have 3 or more grams of fiber per serving, the more fiber, the better. It also helps if the pasta is protein enriched.

Veal Scaloppini
My husband's favorite and so easy!

1 pound thinly sliced veal
½ cup whole-wheat flour
½ teaspoon salt
¼ cup olive oil
1 egg + 2 tablespoons water
1 (10 ¼ ounce) can condensed chicken broth
juice of 1 lemon

Trim the fat, if any, from the veal slices. Pound the veal slices with a meat mallet on both sides to slightly flatten and tenderize.

Combine the flour and salt in a shallow dish

Heat the olive oil in a large skillet over medium-high heat.

Mix the egg and water with a fork. Dip the veal slices in the egg mixture, then in the flour mixture. Place in hot oil and cook just until done, about 2 minutes per side. Place the cooked veal on a warm dish and set aside.

To the skillet drippings, mix in about 1 tablespoon of remaining flour mixture. With a whisk, add the chicken broth. Bring to a boil and reduce the amount by half, about 5 minutes. Reduce the heat to simmer. Add the lemon juice. Serve the sauce over the cooked veal.

Serves 4.

1 serving: Total Fat (g): 15
Protein (g): 18
Total Carbohydrates (g): 3
Dietary Fiber (g): trace
216 calories

Food Exchanges: Lean Meat: 2 ½, Fat: 1½

Grilled Lamb
Savory!

1 (7 - 8 lb.) leg of lamb
1/3 cup Dijon mustard
3 tablespoons olive oil
3 tablespoons soy sauce

Fire up the grill to pre-heat. Keep the heat low or cook indirectly, placing the coals on half of the grill and the lamb on the other half.

Remove the fell (tissue like covering) from the lamb with a sharp knife. Rinse with cool water and pat dry with a paper towel. Make shallow slits on the surface of the lamb with a knife.

In a small bowl, mix the mustard, oil and soy sauce. Rub the mixture onto the lamb. Reserve the extra mixture for basting as lamb cooks.

Place the lamb on a grill and reduce the heat to medium. Insert a thermometer, if desired. Grill, covered, to desired degree of doneness: about 2 hours (140 degrees) for rare, about 2½ hours (160 degrees) for medium, and about 3 hours (170 degrees) for well done. Cooking over indirect heat works best. Just place the hot coals on one side and the meat on the other, not directly over the heat source.

Transfer to a serving platter and let stand about 10 minutes before slicing.

Serves 8.

1 serving: Total Fat (g): 59*
                Protein (g): 57
                Total Carbohydrates (g): 1
                Dietary Fiber (g): trace
                Calories: 829 (before cooking)

Food Exchanges: Lean Meat: 8, Fat: 6½*

*actual fat count is less due to fat that is lost during grilling

Lamb Kabobs
Quick, easy and colorful! Simply delicious for a summer cookout.

1½ pounds lamb (boneless, cut into 1½-inch cubes)
¼ teaspoon salt
1/8 teaspoon black pepper
dash garlic powder
1 medium onion, cut into 1-inch pieces
1 pound cherry tomatoes
olive oil
4 skewers

Combine the spices; sprinkle over the lamb and toss to coat.

Place the lamb, onions and tomatoes on skewers. Brush or spray with olive oil. Place on a hot grill, cooking to desired doneness (10-15 minutes), turning as needed. Remove to a platter and serve.

Serves 4.

1 serving: Total Fat (g): 9
Protein (g): 36
Total Carbohydrates (g): 7
Dietary Fiber (g): 2
270 calories

Food Exchanges: Lean Meat: 5, Vegetables: 1½

Lamb Chops

The recipe allows 2 chops per serving, but if hungry men are present, cook 2½ chops for each person. Accompany the chops with a spinach dish and some colorful marinated vegetables.

4 lamb chops (about 1 pound)
1 teaspoon butter
1/8 teaspoon dried thyme
1/8 teaspoon dried marjoram
black pepper to taste
2 teaspoons soy sauce

Rinse the lamb chops and pat them dry with a paper towel.

Heat a large skillet over medium heat. Melt the butter in the pan; then, add the chops. Sprinkle the lamb chops with the dried thyme and the dried marjoram. Reduce the heat to medium-low heat and cook to desired doneness. Do not allow them to burn or overcook.

Remove the pan from the heat. Remove the lamb chops from the pan and place them on a serving platter.

Add the soy sauce to the pan drippings. Return the pan to low heat and stir to deglaze the pan. Remove from the heat and pour the drippings over the lamb chops.

Serves 2.

1 serving: Total Fat (g): 13
              Protein (g): 38
              Total Carbohydrates (g): 1
              Dietary Fiber: 0
              277 calories

Food Exchanges: Lean Meat: 5½, Fat: ½

Chili Cheese Tart
Serve with dollops of sour cream and avocado salad or as a party appetizer.

Cheddar Pastry
1 cup whole-wheat flour
½ cup oat bran
½ teaspoon salt
½ cup butter, softened
2 cups grated sharp cheddar, room temperature

Filling
½ cup onion, chopped
1 teaspoon olive oil
2 cloves garlic, minced
1 pound ground beef
1 tablespoon chili powder
¼ teaspoon ground cumin
½ teaspoon oregano
½ teaspoon salt
1/8 teaspoon cayenne pepper
1 (15 ounce) can red kidney beans, drained
1 (4 ounce) can green chilies
2 tablespoons kamut flour (spelt or whole wheat flour may be substituted)
1 (8 ounce) can tomato sauce
1 egg
½ cup shredded cheddar

To make the cheese pastry:
Mix the dry ingredients in a medium bowl. Add the softened butter and cheddar and thoroughly mix.

Roll the pastry between 2 sheets of waxed paper until slightly larger than the diameter of the tart pan (quiche or pie pan may be substituted, but cooking time may need to be increased 5-10 minutes).

Remove one side of the paper and place dough-side-down onto the tart pan. Remove the remaining paper and press the dough into place. Trim the edges evenly. Set aside.

Preheat the oven to 450 degrees.

To make the filling:
In a large skillet, heat the oil over medium-high. Add the beef, onions, and garlic. Cook, stirring, until the beef is cooked through and the moisture is gone. Add the spices, kidney beans, and chilies. Reduce the heat to low, stirring as needed.

In a small bowl, combine the tomato sauce, flour, and egg. Beat with a fork until the egg is blended. Stir the tomato mixture into the beef mixture, combining well. Pour the chili mixture into a prepared pastry shell. Top with shredded cheddar.

Place in the preheated oven. Reduce the heat to 350 degrees and bake 20 to 25 minutes or until hot and the cheese topping is golden brown.

Makes 5 to 6 small entrees or 8 to 10 appetizer servings.

1/8 recipe: Total Fat (g): 34
Protein (g): 28
Total Carbohydrates (g): 29
Dietary Fiber (g): 6
514 calories

Food Exchanges: Starch/Bread: 1½, Lean Meat: 3, Vegetable: ½, Fat: 5

Mama's Meat Loaf

1½ pounds lean ground beef
1 (6 ounce) can tomato paste, divided
¼ cup oat bran
¼ cup plain soy milk
1 egg
½ teaspoon salt
dash garlic powder
3 slices Swiss cheese

Preheat the oven to 350 degrees. Grease a loaf pan.

Place the oat bran, milk, egg, salt, garlic powder, and 1 tablespoon of the tomato paste in a medium bowl and mix together.

Add the ground beef and thoroughly mix with a large spoon. Spread half of the meat mixture in a greased loaf pan. Top with the Swiss cheese slices. Spread the remainder of the beef mixture over the cheese. Top with the remaining tomato paste, spreading it over the surface.

Bake for 1 hour. Remove to a serving platter and slice.

Serves 6.

1 serving: Total Fat (g): 40 (before cooking)
Protein (g): 39
Total Carbohydrates (g): 10
Dietary Fiber (g): 2
560 calories (before cooking)

Food Exchanges: Lean Meat: 5, Vegetable: 1, Fat: 5

Mexican Meatloaf
A traditional favorite with South-of-the-Border flavors!

2 teaspoons oat bran
3 tablespoons heavy cream
½ teaspoon salt
1 egg
2 teaspoons olive oil
¼ cup minced onion
1 (4 ounce) can diced green chiles
1¼ pounds lean ground beef
½ cup salsa
½ cup shredded jack-jack cheese

Preheat oven to 350 degrees. Grease or spray loaf pan.

In a medium bowl, combine oat bran, cream, salt and egg. Set aside.

In a small skillet, heat the olive oil over medium heat, then add the onions. Cook just for a few minutes, until the onions are soft and translucent. Remove from heat and stir in the chiles. Set aside.

Add the ground beef to the oat bran mixture, then add the onions and chiles. Combine thoroughly.

Press half of the meat loaf mixture evenly into the bottom of the loaf pan. Spread with salsa; then, place the remaining meat mixture evenly over the top, pressing into place.

Top with shredded cheese. Bake 1 hour.
To serve, remove to platter and slice.

Serves 5.

1 serving: Total Fat (g): 30 (before cooking)
               Protein (g): 22
               Total Carbohydrates (g): 6
               Dietary Fiber (g): 1

Food Exchanges: Lean Meat: 3, Vegetable: ½, Fat: 4 (before cooking)

No-Pasta Lasagna
You can add whole-wheat lasagna noodles, but you really don't need them.

1 medium eggplant
1 pound lean ground beef
2 (10 ounce) packages fresh spinach*
1 small onion, diced
3 cloves garlic, minced
1 teaspoon basil, crushed
1 (28 ounce) can ground or crushed peeled tomatoes
½ teaspoon salt
¼ cup olive oil
2 cups mozzarella cheese, shredded

1 cup ricotta cheese
¼ cup Parmesan cheese

Slice the eggplant lengthwise into 1/4 - inch slices. Sprinkle with salt and set aside.

In a large skillet or pot, brown the ground beef. Add the onions and garlic. Stir on medium heat until the onions are translucent. Add tomatoes, basil, and salt. Cover loosely and simmer 45 minutes to reduce liquid. Stir occasionally to prevent sticking.

Preheat the oven to 350 degrees. Wash and drain the spinach. Blot dry with paper towels. Set aside.

Mix the mozzarella and ricotta. Set aside.

Heat the of olive oil in a skillet. Blot the eggplant dry. Add to the hot oil and fry on each side, turning once when brown. Drain.

Pour the excess oil from the pan. Add the spinach and stir fry until nearly wilted.

In a greased casserole, layer in the following order: one-third of the meat sauce, one-half of the spinach, one-half of the cheese, one-half of the eggplant. Repeat, and then top with the remainder of the meat sauce. Top with grated Parmesan.

Bake 45 minutes.

Serves 8.

1 serving: Total Fat (g): 31
           Protein (g): 25
           Total Carbohydrates (g): 17
           Dietary Fiber (g): 6
           434 calories

Food Exchanges: Lean Meat: 3, Vegetable: 3, Fat: 4½

*3 (10 ounce) packages frozen spinach, thawed and well drained, may be substituted.

Beef Tenderloin with Roasted Garlic Chutney
A very special entree.

6 cloves garlic, roasted
1 (14 ounce) can diced tomatoes, drained
¼ cup balsamic vinegar
1 teaspoon salt
1/8 teaspoon cayenne pepper
2 tablespoons extra virgin olive oil
1 (3 pound) filet of beef (tenderloin)

To roast garlic:
Cut the tip off of each garlic clove. Wrap the garlic in aluminum foil or place in a garlic roaster. Place in the oven and cook at 350 degrees for 30 minutes. Remove and cool.

To make the chutney:
Place the tomatoes in a medium saucepan. Add vinegar, salt, and cayenne pepper. Bring to a boil, then reduce the heat to medium low and simmer for about 30 minutes, stirring as needed. Mixture should be very thick. Set aside to cool.

Squeeze the garlic from the cloves into a processor or blender. Add the olive oil and puree. Stir the garlic mixture into the tomato mixture. Cool completely. May be refrigerated for about 1 month.

To cook the beef:
Up to one hour before roasting, remove the beef from the refrigerator. Trim the fat; sprinkle with salt. Place the meat on a rack in a shallow pan. Spoon about half of the chutney over and press into a thin layer. Reserve the remaining chutney.

Preheat the oven to 450 degrees. Roast the beef for 25 to 30 minutes (120 degrees) for rare or 35 to 40 minutes (130 degrees) for medium rare. Remove from the oven. The temperature will slightly increase after removing. Let the meat rest about 10 minutes before serving. Serve with remaining chutney on the side.

Serves 6.

1 serving: Total Fat (g): 57
              Protein (g): 41
              Total Carbohydrates (g): 5
              Dietary Fiber (g): 1
              703 calories

Food Exchanges: Starch/Bread: 1, Lean Meat: 5½, Vegetable: 1, Fat: 8

Flank Steak Stuffed with Spinach & Sun Dried Tomatoes
This scrumptious and easy recipe is nice enough for guests, but easy enough to make for a family dinner.

1½ pounds flank steak
10 ounces frozen whole leaf spinach
¼ cup crumbled traditional feta cheese
½ cup julienned sundried tomatoes in oil
4 slices provolone cheese (about ¼ pound)

Preheat the oven to 375 degrees.

Spray or oil a loaf pan with olive oil and set aside.

Using a meat mallet, pound the flank steak to about ¾ inches thick. Set the steak aside until ready to fill. It will be more tender if you allow it to reach room temperature while you are preparing the filling.

To prepare the filling, thaw the spinach by microwaving or by placing the spinach in a sieve and running hot water over. Either way, squeeze all excess water from the spinach by using a colander, sieve, or paper towels. Spread the spinach evenly over the flank steak, staying about ½ inch from the edges of the meat.

Sprinkle the crumbled feta cheese evenly over the spinach. Then, layer the sun dried tomatoes over the feta. Top all with the sliced provolone cheese.

Roll the steak lengthwise, jellyroll fashion and lay seam side down in the prepared loaf pan. If you choose to cook this in a larger pan, you may need to wrap the rolled steak with unflavored dental floss or kitchen twine. Drizzle any remaining olive oil from the sun dried tomatoes over the top or brush with olive oil.

Bake for 1 hour. Remove from the oven and let stand for 10 minutes before slicing

Serves 5.

1 serving: Total Fat (g): 24
             Protein (g): 35
             Total Carbohydrates (g): 2
             Dietary Fiber (g): 2
             377 calories

Total Exchanges: Vegetable: ½, Lean Meat: 4½, Fat: 2

Steak Fajitas
Serve with sides of shredded lettuce, shredded cheese, sour cream and guacamole.

Fajita Marinade
½ cup red wine vinegar
3 tablespoons canola oil
juice of 2 limes (about 1/3 cup)
1 tablespoon Worcestershire sauce
1 teaspoon chili powder
½ teaspoon ground cumin
½ teaspoon black pepper
1 jalapeno pepper, seeded and minced
¼ cup minced onion
1 clove garlic, finely minced

1 ¼ pound skirt steak
1 tablespoon olive oil
1 large sweet onion
2 poblano or bell peppers (depending on the amount of heat desired) seeded and sliced

The day before, mix all the marinade ingredients (the first ten ingredients) in a non-metal baking dish or container. Add the skirt steak and cover the container tightly. Refrigerate overnight. It works well to place the marinade and steak together in a large zip-lock bag and refrigerate until ready to use.

30 minutes before cooking your fajitas, heat the grill. While the grill is heating, slice the peppers in half and remove the seeds with the edge of a spoon. Cut the peppers into thin slices. Slice the onion into thin slices, as well.

In a large skillet, heat the olive oil over medium heat. Add the onions and sliced peppers, stirring as needed. Remove from heat when the onions become fragrant and begin to caramelize (brown).

10 minutes before serving, place the steak on the grill and cook to desired doneness. Remove to a platter and slice <u>across the grain</u> of the meat. Add the cooked onions and peppers and serve with low carb tortillas and condiments.

Serves 4.

1 serving (not including tortillas): Total Fat (g): 29 (includes all marinade – actual count is lower)
Protein (g): 29
Total Carbohydrates (g): 12
Dietary Fiber (g): 2
408 calories (includes all marinade – actual count is lower)

Food Exchanges (not including tortillas): Lean Meat: 4, Fat: 3½

Be sure to have your condiment dishes prepared before grilling the meat.

Pepper Roasted Tenderloin

1 beef tenderloin roast, ready to cook (about 1½ pounds)
1 teaspoon freshly ground black peppercorns (black pepper may be substituted, but is not as zippy)
½ teaspoon salt
1 tablespoon olive oil
1 clove garlic, crushed

Preheat the oven to 425 degrees.

Combine salt and ground pepper. Set aside.

Combine the garlic with the olive oil. Rub the oil mixture over the entire roast, and then rub the salt and pepper mixture into the roast. Place in greased a casserole that will allow for the length of the roast.

Bake, uncovered for 10 minutes. Reduce heat to 375 degrees. Roast to internal temperature of 140 degrees (rare), about 20 minutes additional time (30 minutes total).

Serves 6.

1 serving: Total Fat (g): 10
                Protein (g): 24
                Total Carbohydrates (g): trace
                Dietary Fiber (g): trace
                193 calories

Food Exchanges: Lean Meat: 3 ½, Fat: ½

Oven Roasted Flank Steak

1 (1¼ pound) flank steak
1 tablespoon butter, softened
¼ cup chopped onion
1/8 teaspoon black pepper
¼ teaspoon salt
non-stick spray

Preheat oven to 350 degrees. Spray the roasting pan with non-stick spray.

Rub the softened butter over the surfaces of meat. Place the meat in a pan and sprinkle with salt and pepper. Add the onions to the bottom of the pan around the meat so that the onions will caramelize.

Bake 350 degrees for 2 hours or until the juices are brown and mostly cooked away.

Serves 4.

1 serving: Total Fat (g): 16
Protein (g): 28
Total Carbohydrates (g): 1
Dietary Fiber (g): trace
263 calories

Food Exchanges: Lean Meat: 4, Fat: 1

Badlands Beef
Try it with a nice salad and Spanish rice.

1½ pounds lean stew beef
½ large sweet onion
3 jalapeno peppers, seeded
1 clove garlic
2 tablespoons olive oil
non-stick spray
½ teaspoon salt
1/8 teaspoon pepper

Spray an 8-inch square casserole with non-stick spray.

Slice the onion into long, thin slices. Layer over the bottom of the casserole. Top with beef.

Mince the peppers, being careful not to touch your face or eyes. Place over the beef. Sprinkle with salt and pepper.

Crush the garlic; combine with the oil. Drizzle oil over all. Cover the casserole with foil, turning one corner up to vent and allow evaporation.

Bake at 350 degrees for 1½ to 2 hours or until the liquid is nearly gone and bottom is browned.

Serves 4.

1 serving: Total Fat (g): 31
                Protein (g): 34
                Total Carbohydrates (g): 4
                Dietary Fiber (g): 1
                432 calories

Food Exchanges: Lean Meat: 4½, Vegetable: 1, Fat: 3

Marinated Steak Salad
A touch of Asian flavor.

4 delmonico (rib eye) steaks (½ pounds each)

Marinade
1 cup red wine
3 tablespoons soy sauce
1 teaspoon ginger, freshly grated
4 cloves garlic, minced
2 tablespoons onion, finely minced
¼ teaspoon red pepper flakes

Dressing
2 tablespoons red wine vinegar
2 teaspoons soy sauce
½ teaspoon dried mustard
1 clove garlic, minced
1 tablespoon onion, finely minced
½ teaspoon dried cilantro
½ cup sesame oil

Salad Ingredients
6 cups greens, such as romaine, spinach, and/or leaf lettuce

To assemble:
Mix the marinade ingredients. Add the steaks and marinate, covered, for 1 hour at room temperature.

Mix the dressing and set aside.

Grill or broil the steaks to desired doneness, brushing with marinade.

Divide the greens among 4 plates. When the steaks are ready, remove from the grill, let them stand for a minute or two, then slice into ¼ inch slices. Arrange the steak on top of the greens. Top with dressing.

Serves 4.

1 serving (not including marinade):

Total Fat (g): 48
Protein (g): 49
Total Carbohydrates (g): 5
Dietary Fiber (g): 3
654 calories

Food Exchanges: Lean Meat: 6½, Vegetable: 1, Fat: 7

Poultry

Parmesan Chicken
Better than fried.

4 chicken breast halves, skinless and boneless
¼ cup melted butter or olive oil
¼ cup Parmesan cheese, grated
2 wafers of fiber rye crisp bread, broken into small pieces

Preheat the oven to 325 degrees. Wash the chicken, remove the fat and gristle and set aside.

Combine the cheese and crisp bread pieces in a food processor or blender until evenly mixed. Pour into a dish.

Dip the chicken in oil or butter, then in cheese mixture. Place on a greased oven-safe dish. Bake for 35 minutes.

Serves 4.

1 serving: Total Fat (g): 17
                  Protein (g): 29
                  Total Carbohydrates (g): 2
                  Dietary Fiber (g): 1
                  Calories: 301

Food Exchanges: Lean Meat: 4, Fat: 2½

Tomato Olive Chicken Bake

Scrumptious and filling, dotted with festive Spanish olives, this low-carb casserole makes a terrific supper. All you need is a tossed green salad!

2 tablespoons oat bran
4 chicken breast halves
2 tablespoons soy flour
2 teaspoons wheat bran
3 tablespoons olive oil
¼ cup diced onions
1 clove garlic, minced
½ cup sliced green olives
1 (14.5 ounce) can diced tomatoes
¼ teaspoon ground cloves
¼ teaspoon crushed red pepper
½ teaspoon oregano
1 cup shredded jack-jack cheese, divided

Heat the oven to 325 degrees. Spray a 9 x 13 inch baking dish with non-stick spray or grease with olive oil. Sprinkle the oat bran over the bottom of the dish. Set aside.

Place the soy flour and wheat bran in a paper or plastic bag; shake to mix; add the chicken and shake to coat.

In a large skillet, heat the oil over medium heat. Add the chicken and sear about 1 minute on each side. Remove to the baking dish. Set aside.

Immediately add the onions to the hot skillet and cook until translucent. Add the garlic, then the olives, tomatoes, cloves, pepper, oregano and ½ cup of the shredded cheese. Stir to heat. Remove from heat and pour the tomato mixture over the chicken. Top with the remaining ½ cup cheese.

Bake 35 to 40 minutes, until hot and bubbly and cheese begins to brown.

Serves 4.

1 serving: Total Fat (g): 35
               Protein (g): 39
               Total Carbohydrates (g): 9
               Dietary Fiber (g): 3
               395 calories

Food Exchanges: Lean Meat: 5½, Vegetable: 1, Fat: 3½

Chicken Enchiladas

1 tablespoon olive oil
¼ cup diced onion
1 (14½ ounce) can diced tomatoes
1 (4 ounce) can green chilies
1 small clove garlic
¼ teaspoon salt
¼ teaspoon dried oregano
3 cooked, skinned, boneless chicken breasts
8 low carb tortillas (whole wheat tortillas may be used, but will raise carb count a bit)
1 cup shredded jack-jack cheese
sour cream
guacamole
Lettuce and tomato, optional

Preheat the oven to 350 degrees.

To make the enchilada sauce, sauté the onion in the oil until crisp-tender. Add the tomatoes, chilies, garlic, salt and oregano. Bring to a boil. Puree to a coarse texture. Set aside.

Chop the chicken into small pieces. This is easiest when done in a food processor. Mix with a small amount of enchilada sauce and half of cheese.

Spoon the chicken mixture along center of each tortilla. Roll up, leaving ends open. Place each in a greased casserole, seam side down. Pour the remaining sauce over the top and sprinkle with remaining cheese.

Bake 30 minutes, until hot and bubbly.

Serves 8.

1 serving: Total Fat (g): 10
            Protein (g): 30
            Total Carbohydrates (g): 16
            Dietary Fiber (g): 10
            253 calories

Food Exchanges: Lean Meat: 3, Vegetable: ½, Fat: 1

Serve with guacamole and sour cream. Garnish with shredded lettuce and tomato, if desired.

Baked Chicken Burritos
A delicious dish everyone will enjoy, with classic Mexican ingredients.

5 (6-inch) whole wheat tortillas
2 cups cooked, lean chicken, chopped
2 tablespoons olive oil
1 cup onion, chopped
1 jalapeno pepper, seeded and minced
1 clove garlic, crushed
1 (14.5 ounce) can diced tomatoes
1 teaspoon cocoa
½ teaspoon oregano
½ teaspoon cumin
¼ teaspoon salt
1 cup Colby-jack cheese, shredded and divided

Take the tortillas from the refrigerator to bring to room temperature. Preheat the oven to 350 degrees. Grease a 2 quart baking dish and set aside. Place the cut-up chicken in a large bowl.

In a medium saucepan, heat the oil over medium heat. Add the onions, pepper and garlic. Stir until the onion becomes translucent. Add the tomatoes, cocoa, oregano, cumin, and salt. Bring to a boil and remove from heat.

Using a slotted spoon, take about ¾ cup of the tomato mixture from the pot and add to the chicken. Add ¼ cup of the cheese and toss all together until evenly combined.

Spoon a small portion of the tomato mixture into the bottom of the baking dish to just cover the bottom. Divide the chicken mixture evenly among the 5 tortillas. Fold each tortilla together from each end, overlapping in the middle, making a square "package" to hold the chicken. Place each folded-side-down in the casserole, pressing them together to fit. Spoon the remaining tomato mixture over the top; top with remaining cheese.

Bake about 20 minutes, until the cheese is melted and the burritos are heated through.

Serves 5 hungry people.

1 serving: Total Fat (g): 18
               Protein (g): 29
               Total Carbohydrates (g): 20
               Dietary Fiber (g): 11
               327 calories

Food Exchanges: Lean Meat: 3, Vegetable: 1½, Fat: 2

Chicken Divan
Easy to prepare and great for a buffet dish

Non-stick spray
1 (1¼ pound) package chicken breast tenderloins
1 pound fresh broccoli
3 tablespoons butter, divided
3 tablespoons whole wheat or kamut flour
1 (10¼ ounce) can double strength chicken broth
2 cups half & half
½ teaspoon salt
1/8 teaspoon ground mace
½ cup Swiss cheese
1 cup soft whole grain breadcrumbs (about 4 slices bread)
¼ cup chopped pecans

Spray an 8 x 8 inch casserole with non-stick spray. Preheat the oven to 350 degrees.

Rinse the chicken, pat dry, and remove any fat deposits. Layer across the bottom of the casserole.

Rinse the broccoli; remove the woody ends, so that spears are about 4 inches in length. Slice the spears lengthwise so that they may be easily layered. Arrange on top of the chicken in a single layer. Set aside.

In a medium saucepan, melt <u>2 tablespoons</u> butter over medium heat. Whisk in flour, salt, and mace. Whisk in the chicken broth, then the half & half. Bring to a boil. Reduce the heat to medium, stirring constantly, until the mixture thickens. Remove from the heat and stir in the cheese. Pour mixture evenly over the broccoli and chicken. Cover with foil. Bake 45 minutes at 350 degrees.

Meanwhile, melt the remaining 1-tablespoon butter in a small skillet and add pecans and breadcrumbs, tossing to coat. Remove from heat.

After the first 45 of baking, top the casserole with the breadcrumb mixture. Return to the oven for 15 minutes, until the top is toasty brown.

Serves 4.

1 serving: Total Fat (g): 35
              Protein (g): 51
              Total Carbohydrates (g): 37
              Dietary Fiber (g): 8
              665 calories

  Food Exchanges: Starch/Bread: 1½, Lean Meat: 5, Vegetable: 1, Non-fat milk: ½, Fat: 6

Chicken Stroganoff
A different take on an old favorite.

3 cups cooked brown or wild rice
2 whole boneless, skinned chicken breasts, cut into strips
dash garlic powder
¼ teaspoon poultry seasoning
¼ teaspoon black pepper
3 tablespoons soy sauce
½ pound mushrooms, sliced
2 tablespoons butter, divided
2 tablespoons whole-wheat flour
2 cups sour cream

Melt 1 tablespoon butter. Add the chicken, garlic powder, poultry seasoning, and black pepper. Sprinkle with the soy sauce and sauté over medium heat just until the chicken is cooked through. Remove from the pan.

Add the mushrooms to the hot pan. Sauté until cooked through. Remove to a dish separate from the chicken.

Melt the remaining 1 tablespoon butter to the hot pan; stir in the flour. Add ½ cup water, stirring with a whisk. Let thicken and salt to taste, stirring as needed. Add the chicken. Simmer over lowest heat for 10 minutes. Remove from the heat. Add the mushrooms and sour cream. Serve with the cooked whole grain rice.

Serves 5.

1 serving: Total Fat (g): 28 (brown rice), 27 (wild rice)
                Protein (g): 29 (brown rice), 30 (wild rice)
                Total Carbohydrates (g): 37 (brown rice), 29 (wild rice)
                Dietary Fiber (g): 3
                476 calories

Food Exchanges: Starch/Bread: 2, Lean Meat: 3, Vegetable: ½, Non-fat milk: ½, Fat: 5

Spinach Stuffed Chicken Breasts

A lovely and special entrée, this dish is very nice with a colorful salad and a bit of whole grain bread.

3 tablespoons olive oil
½ cup minced onion
4 cups fresh washed spinach (about 1 package)
1 (4 ounce) package feta cheese
4 slices bacon
4 chicken breast halves

Preheat the oven to 350 degrees.
Shred the spinach by rolling up and slicing into strips with a sharp knife.

In a skillet, heat the oil. Add the onion and spinach; sauté until the onion is translucent. Reduce heat to medium and cook until the spinach is reduced in volume and all water is cooked out.

While the spinach is cooking, use a meat mallet to gently pound the chicken to about 1/8 inch thickness. It helps to cover the chicken with plastic wrap before pounding the meat in order to prevent splatters.

After removing the spinach from the heat, toss in the feta cheese.

Divide the spinach mixture by placing a portion in the center of each chicken breast. Wrap each chicken breast gently around the spinach mixture. Place folded-side-down on greased casserole. Cut each bacon slice in half and place and cover each chicken breast with two halves of bacon. Bake 35 minutes, and then place under the broiler 5 minutes to crisp the bacon, being careful not to burn.

Serves 4.

1 serving: Total Fat (g): 18
                Protein (g): 32
                Total Carbohydrates (g): 3
                Dietary Fiber (g): 1
                354 calories

Food Exchanges: Lean Meat: 4½, Vegetable ½, Fat: 3

* If made earlier in the day, completely cool the spinach mixture before stuffing the chicken. Refrigerate until ready to bake, adding about 5 minutes to the baking time.

Diablo Chicken
Adjust heat to individual taste.

4 chicken breast halves, skinned and boned
juice of one lime (about 2 tablespoon)
1 tablespoon olive oil
dash Tabasco
2 cloves garlic, crushed
¼ - ½ teaspoon cayenne pepper
¼ ½ teaspoon black pepper
½ teaspoon salt

Mix all ingredients except chicken in a ceramic or plastic dish. Add the chicken, turning once. Cover and refrigerate at least 30 minutes.

Grill or broil until the chicken is cooked through, basting as needed.

Serves 4.

1 serving: Total Fat (g): 6
Protein (g): 26
Total Carbohydrates (g): 1
Dietary Fiber (g): trace
174 calories

Food Exchanges: Lean Meat: 3½, Fat: ½

Mexicali Chicken

4 chicken breast fillets
1 tablespoon chili powder
2 tablespoons olive oil
1 large sweet onion, diced
1 jalapeno pepper, seeded and minced
2-3 tomatoes, seeded and diced
1 small bunch cilantro, washed and minced (about 2 tablespoons)
½ teaspoon salt

Wash the chicken fillets and pat dry. Sprinkle both sides with chili powder.

Heat the oil in a large skillet over medium heat. Add the diced onions and minced jalapeno. Stir until translucent. Push the onions to the side of the skillet. Add the chicken breasts and reduce heat to medium-low. Turn over when cooked halfway through. Cook 2 to 3 minutes.

Pour the tomatoes over the onions. Add the cilantro and salt. Gently stir into the onions and tomatoes. Continue cooking until the vegetables are heated through and the chicken is done. Remove to warm platter and serve.

Serves 4.

1 serving: Total Fat (g): 10
            Protein (g): 28
            Total Carbohydrates (g): 8
            Dietary Fiber (g): 2
            236 calories

Food Exchanges: Lean Meat: 3½, Vegetable: 1, Fat: 1½

Italian Baked Chicken

This dish makes a nice meal when served with a double portion of green veggies.

4 boned, skinless chicken breast halves
1 cup Caesar Cardini's Italian dressing (or other sugar free Italian salad dressing)
½ cup grated Parmesan cheese
½ cup oat bran

Place the chicken breasts in a medium bowl. Pour the dressing over and marinate about 30 minutes in refrigerator.

Preheat the oven to 425 degrees.

In a small bowl, combine Parmesan cheese and oat bran.

Remove the chicken from the marinade one piece at a time. Roll each piece in the cheese mixture. Place in a greased casserole dish. Place in the preheated oven. Reduce the oven heat to 325 degrees. Bake 45 minutes.

Serves 4.

1 serving: Total Fat (g): 9
               Protein (g): 33
               Carbohydrates (g): 0
               Dietary Fiber (g): 2

Food Exchanges: Starch/Bread: ½, Lean Meat: 4½, Fat: 1

Olive Chicken
Festive and delicious!

3 tablespoons whole grain flour
¾ teaspoon paprika
4 chicken breast halves, boned and skinned
2 tablespoons olive oil
1 medium onion, thinly sliced
3 cloves garlic, minced
1 (15 ounce) can chicken broth
1¼ teaspoons dried basil
1/8 teaspoon pepper
1½ teaspoons lemon juice
¾ cup sliced green stuffed olives
8 ounces button mushrooms, halved
1/3 cup dry, white wine
2 cups cooked brown or wild rice (long cooking)

Mix 2 tablespoons flour with the paprika. Dredge the chicken in the flour mixture.

In a large skillet, heat the oil. Add the chicken and brown on both sides. Remove the chicken.

Sauté the garlic and onion until lightly browned. Stir in the chicken broth, basil, pepper, and lemon juice. Bring to a boil. Add wine, olive, mushrooms, and chicken. Cover and simmer over very low heat for 20 to 25 minutes, until tender. Remove the chicken and vegetables to a serving dish with a slotted spoon.

Blend the remaining 1 tablespoon flour and 2 tablespoons water. Add to the liquid in the pan. Thicken over medium-low heat, stirring. Pour over the chicken and serve.

Serves 4.

1 serving: Total Fat (g): 14
          Protein (g): 33 (brown rice), 34 (wild rice)
          Total Carbohydrates (g): 35 (brown rice), 29 (wild rice)
          Dietary Fiber (g): 4
          Calories: 414 (brown rice); 388 (wild rice)

Food Exchanges: Starch/Bread: 1½ (wild rice) 2 (brown rice), Lean Meat: 4, Vegetable: 1, Fat: 2

Chicken Bourguignon
A hearty dish for a company meal!

6 chicken breast halves, skinned and boned
4 tablespoons butter
½ pound sliced mushrooms
1 medium onion, diced
1 bay leaf
1 clove garlic, crushed
½ teaspoon dried thyme
1 tablespoon whole-wheat flour
½ cup chicken broth
1 cup Burgundy wine

Sprinkle the chicken with salt and pepper.

Melt the butter; add the chicken. Brown on each side, reduce the heat to low, and cook 15 minutes. Put the chicken pieces on a dish and cover to keep warm.

Add the mushrooms to the pan; cook on medium high 2 minutes. Add the onion, garlic, thyme, and bay leaf. Cook, stirring, for 2 minutes. Sprinkle with flour, and then add the broth and wine, stirring to blend.

Add the chicken and juices. Serve with sauce over whole grain noodles or brown rice.

Serves 6.

1 serving: Total Fat (g): 11
Protein (g): 28
Total Carbohydrates (g): 5
Dietary Fiber (g): 1
243 calories

Food Exchanges: Lean Meat: 3½, Vegetable: ½, Fat: 1½

Chicken with Broccoli
A quick and healthy supper! Just add a salad.

1 pound fresh broccoli or 2 (10 ounces) boxes frozen broccoli
2 tablespoons whole wheat flour*
1½ teaspoon salt
½ teaspoon tarragon
4 chicken breast halves or 6 chicken thighs, skinned
2 tablespoons olive oil
1 tablespoon lemon juice
½ cup sour cream
½ cup plain fat yogurt
2 tablespoons shredded sharp cheese

Preheat the oven to 350 degrees. Spray or oil an ovenproof casserole dish.

Wash and cut the broccoli into spears. Cover with plastic wrap, leaving one edge open for venting. Microwave for 2 minutes. Set aside.

Place the flour, salt, and tarragon in a plastic or paper bag. Add the chicken the chicken to the mixture and shake until the chicken is coated evenly.

Heat the oil in a skillet. Add the chicken and brown on both sides. Arrange in the casserole dish. Top with the broccoli. Set aside.

To the pan juices, add lemon juice, sour cream, and remaining flour mixture. Stir and pour over the chicken and broccoli. Top with the cheese.

Bake at 350 degrees for 30 minutes.

Serves 4.

*Spelt or kamut flour may be substituted.

1 serving: Total Fat (g): 17
                    Protein (g): 33
                    Total Carbohydrates (g): 9
                    Dietary Fiber (g): 3
                    327 calories

Food Exchanges: Lean Meat: 4, Vegetable: ½, Fat: 3

Chicken with Tomatoes & Kalamata Olives

A scrumptious Mediterranean chicken dish. Try this easy and tasty entree with a side of grilled veggies!

1 small head garlic
½ cup kalamata olives, halved and pitted
1 (15 ounce) can diced tomatoes
½ teaspoon dried basil
pinch of crushed red pepper (optional)
4 boneless, skinless chicken breast halves
3 tablespoons whole grain flour
½ teaspoon salt
¼ cup olive oil

To roast the garlic:

Remove most of the outer skins. Cut about ¼ inch from the tops of the bulbs. Drizzle or spray with oil and either place in a garlic roaster or wrap in foil. Bake about 45 minutes. Remove from oven; remove cover and let cool.

Halve and pit the olives, if necessary. Place the olives in a small saucepan with the diced tomatoes, basil and red pepper. Simmer for about 30 minutes, cooking out the liquid.

With the flat side of a meat mallet, lightly pound the chicken breasts to an even thickness, about ½ inch.

In a shallow dish or in a paper bag, combine the flour and salt.

In a large frying pan, heat the oil over medium-low heat, being careful not to overheat.

Lightly dip the chicken pieces in the flour mixture or shake in the bag to coat. Cook in the oil, turning after chicken is cooked about half through. When done, remove chicken to a platter and keep warm.

Pour the tomato mixture into pan with chicken drippings. Stir over low heat long enough to deglaze the pan. Spoon over chicken and serve.

Serves 4.

1 serving: Total Fat (g): 20
                Protein (g): 29
                Total Carbohydrates (g): 11
                Dietary Fiber (g): 2
                380 calories

Food Exchanges: Starch/Bread: ½, Lean Meat: 4, Vegetable: 1, Fat: 3½

Chicken Kabobs with Grilled Asparagus

1 pound fresh asparagus

¼ cup sesame oil
1 tablespoon soy sauce
1 tablespoon sherry
1 tablespoon sesame seeds

1 pound shiitake mushrooms (or mushrooms of choice)
1 medium onion, cut into 1½ inch squares
4 chicken breast halves, cut into 1½ inch cubes

Snap the woody ends from the asparagus; clean and remove the nubs from stalk, if desired. Spray or brush with olive oil. Set aside.

Prepare the marinade in a medium bowl by combining the sesame oil, seeds, soy sauce and sherry. Reserve 2 tablespoons in a smaller bowl and toss the onions and mushrooms in a smaller bowl to coat. Set aside.

Gently toss the chicken pieces with the marinade in a medium bowl and refrigerate for 15 to 30 minutes, until ready to cook.

Arrange the chicken, onions, and mushrooms on a skewer. Place on a medium hot grill. Place the asparagus spears on grill at the same time. Cook until the chicken is done, turning as needed, about 15 to 20 minutes. Do not overcook. Arrange on a serving dish and enjoy.

Makes 4 servings.

1 serving: Total Fat (g): 11
                Protein (g): 30
                Total Carbohydrates (g): 13
                Dietary Fiber (g): 3
                274 calories

Food Exchanges: Lean Meat: 3½, Vegetable: 2, Fat: 1½

Turkey Breast with Wild Rice Stuffing
Don't wait for the holidays to enjoy this tasty dish!

1 whole turkey breast, uncooked (about 3 pounds)
½ cup wild rice
1 (14½ ounce) can chicken broth
¼ cup butter
½ cup celery, chopped
¼ cup onion, chopped
1 teaspoon poultry seasoning
½ teaspoon salt
2 cups bread crumbs, made from whole grain bread, torn or chopped in a processor

Bring the chicken broth to boil in a medium saucepan. Add the wild rice and reduce the heat to medium-low. Cover. Cook for 50 minutes. Do not drain. Set aside.

Preheat the oven to 350 degrees.

Rinse the turkey breast in cool water; pat dry and place in a roasting pan.

Sauté the onion and celery in the butter until tender and translucent. Mix with the wild rice. Add the poultry seasoning and salt. Gently mix the breadcrumbs into the rice mixture. Spoon the stuffing <u>underneath</u> turkey breast. It is important to keep the rice moist. Otherwise, it will become crunchy. Loosely cover any exposed stuffing with foil. Brush the top of turkey with butter or olive oil.

Roast the turkey breast according to instructions on package, about 1 hour.

Serves 6 - 8.

1/6 recipe: Total Fat (g): 24
              Protein (g): 51
              Total Carbohydrates (g): 25
              Dietary Fiber (g): 3
              582 calories

Food Exchanges: Starch/Bread: 1½, Lean Meat: 6½, Vegetable: ½, Fat: 2

Tex-Mex Turkey Salad

This recipe is nice to make ahead of time, giving the spicy flavors of the dressing time to develop. The Tex-Mex Mayo is also a nice "bread spread" to make for turkey or chicken sandwiches.

Tex-Mex Mayo

¼ cup mayonnaise
½ teaspoon chili powder
¼ teaspoon ground cumin
1 teaspoon lime juice
½ teaspoon salt, to taste
1 tablespoon fresh, chopped cilantro (optional)

Salad Ingredients

2 cups cooked turkey, cut into ½ inch cubes
½ medium avocado (about ½ cup cubed)
1 ripe small tomato, seeded and diced (about ½ cup)
2 tablespoons red onion, diced

In a small bowl, mix together the mayonnaise, chili powder, ground cumin, the lime juice, salt. If you are using cilantro, wash, drain and pat it dry. Chop the leaves, discarding excessive stems. Add to the mayonnaise mixture. Refrigerate until you are ready to serve the salad.

Place the cooked, cubed turkey in a medium bowl. Cut the tomato in half, scoop out the seeds with your fingers and discard the seeds. Dice the remaining "meat" of the tomato. Add to the bowl with the turkey and the avocado. Dice the onion and add to the bowl. Cut the avocado in half, twist; and then pull apart. Spray the half that holds the seed with oil and place in the refrigerator for use later. Peel the remaining avocado half and dice. Add to the rest.

Pour the Tex-Mex Mayo over the turkey mixture and gently stir to coat the turkey and vegetables with the dressing. Refrigerate until ready to serve.

Serves 4.

1 serving: Total Fat (g): 19
            Protein (g): 19
            Total Carbohydrates (g): 3
            Dietary Fiber (g): 1
            259 calories

Food Exchanges: Lean Meat: 2½, Vegetable: ½, Fat: 1½

Side Dishes

Texas Onion Rings

2 large sweet onions, cut into 3-inch rings
1½ cups whole-wheat flour
¼ cup chili powder
1½ teaspoons salt
1½ teaspoons ground cumin
1 teaspoon paprika
1 egg, beaten with 2 tablespoons water
½ cup vegetable oil, preferably olive oil or unprocessed coconut oil

Mix the egg and water together in large bowl. Toss the onions into mixture and stir until the rings are coated with egg mixture. Set aside.

Mix the dry ingredients in a medium bowl.

Heat the oil to 360 degrees (till hot and a water droplet sizzles) on medium heat.

Remove the rings from the egg mixture in small batches and dredge in the flour mixture. Add to the hot oil, turning once, about 45 seconds cooking time. Transfer to paper towels to drain. Serve immediately.

Serves 6.

1 serving: Total Fat (g): 11*
               Protein (g): 6
               Total Carbohydrates (g): 28
               Dietary Fiber (g): 6
               Calories: 226*

Food Exchanges: Starch/Bread: 1½, Vegetable: 1/2, Fat: 2*

includes all vegetable oil for frying

Stuffed Banana Peppers

This is a nice recipe for making ahead of time. Just keep in the refrigerator until ready to bake.

8 large sweet banana peppers
2 teaspoons olive oil
½ cup diced onion
1 jalapeno pepper
1 medium-sized ripe tomato
1½ cups Colby or Monterey Jack Cheese, grated
1/8 teaspoon salt
8 slices bacon (sugar-free if possible)

Preheat the oven to 400 degrees. Grease the top rack of your broiler pan.

Slit each pepper lengthwise. With the edge of a small spoon, gently scrape out the seeds and wash. Set aside to drain.

Slice the jalapeno pepper in half lengthwise, then scrape out the seeds and trim the stem away. Discard the stem and seeds. Be careful not to touch your face or eyes and wear protective gloves if your skin is sensitive. Mince the jalapeno into very small pieces. Set aside.

In a small skillet, heat the olive oil. Add the onion and minced jalapeno and cook just until the onion is translucent. Remove from the heat and set aside.

If desired, peel the tomato. Cut the tomato in half; remove the seedy pulp and discard. Discard the stem end. Finely dice the remaining "meat" of the tomato.

In a small bowl, mix the grated cheese with the tomato, onion and jalapeno, and salt. Divide the mixture among the 8 peppers, stuffing each pepper with the mixture.

Wrap each stuffed pepper with a piece of bacon from top to bottom and secure the bacon with a wooden toothpick. Place each on the greased rack of a broiler pan and bake for about 35 minutes, or until the bacon is crisp.

Serves 8.

1 serving (before cooking): Total Fat (g): 11
Protein (g): 8
Total Carbohydrates (g): 5
Dietary Fiber (g): 2
150 calories

Food Exchanges: Lean Meat: 1, Vegetable: 1, Fat: 1½

Artichoke Stuffed Tomatoes

Try this dish with red vine-ripened summer tomatoes. Stuffed with artichoke hearts, this dish is easy and elegant to serve. Delicious in the oven or cooked on the grill!

6 large ripe tomatoes
1 (14 ounce) can artichoke hearts, drained and rinsed
2 ounces cream cheese
¼ cup Parmesan cheese, grated

Preheat oven to 400 degrees.

Cut tops from tomatoes. Carefully remove pulp with fingers, then remove core with sharp knife, being careful to leave the bottom of the tomato intact. Place in a greased baking dish.

In a medium bowl, mash artichoke hearts with cream cheese and Parmesan cheese. Press gently into the tomato shells, mounding any excess mixture on top. Sprinkle each with Parmesan cheese.

Bake at 400 degrees for about 35 minutes or until tops are lightly browned.

These may also be cooked on a covered, medium-hot grill, but place around edges rather than directly over flame.

Serve on a lettuce lined dish for a pretty presentation. Serves 6.

1 serving: Total Fat (g): 5
         Protein (g): 5
         Total Carbohydrates (g): 13
         Dietary Fiber (g): 5
         107 calories

Food Exchanges: Lean Meat: ½, Vegetable: 2½, Fat ½

Red Cabbage
Perfect with pork

1 tablespoon bacon fat
1 small head red cabbage, thinly sliced
1 large onion, thinly sliced
½ teaspoon salt
¼ cup red wine vinegar
3 tablespoons fructose or agave syrup (1/4 cup alternative granular sweetener may be substituted)

Place the cabbage in a large bowl and cover with water. Set aside.

Heat the bacon fat in large, heavy pot. Add the onions and cook over medium heat until the onions are tender and begin to brown.

 Drain the cabbage. Add to the pot with onions. Add 3 cups of water, salt, vinegar, and fructose (or sweetener). Bring to a boil, loosely cover, then simmer for 50 to 60 minutes, until the cabbage is tender and the water is nearly cooked out.

Serves 8.

1 serving: Total Fat (g): 2
         Protein (g): trace
         Total Carbohydrates (g): 9
         Dietary Fiber (g): trace
         49 calories

Food Exchanges: Vegetable: ½, Fat: ½, Other Carb: ½

Red Cabbage with Cranberries

1 small head red cabbage (about 8 cups)
1 tablespoon olive oil
1 large onion, thinly sliced
1 cup dried cranberries
3 cups water
½ teaspoon salt
¼ cup red wine vinegar
¼ cup agave nectar (or 1/3 cup Splenda or alternative granular sweetener)
½ cup orange juice
½ teaspoon allspice
¼ teaspoon cloves

Core the cabbage; shred or chop and place in a bowl. Cover the cabbage with cold water. Set aside.

In a large pot, heat the olive oil over medium heat. Add the onion and cook until translucent. Add the remaining ingredients. Bring to a boil, and then reduce heat to low, simmering for 50 minutes to an hour. Stir occasionally. Cabbage will be tender and most of the water will be cooked out.

Serves 10.

1 serving: Total Fat (g): 2
              Protein (g): 1
              Total Carbohydrates (g): 15
              Dietary Fiber (g): 2
              65 calories

Food Exchanges: Vegetable: 1, Fat: ½, Other Carbs: ½

Southern Summer Squash

2 tablespoons butter
1 large sweet onion, sliced into rings
8 yellow summer squash, sliced
½ teaspoon salt
1/8 teaspoon pepper

Melt the butter in a skillet. Add the other ingredients. Cook over medium heat until the squash cooks down and the onion begins to brown, stirring occasionally, about 30 minutes.

When done, the squash is soft and takes on a golden color.

Serves 4.

1 serving: Total Fat (g): 6
          Protein (g): 3
          Total Carbohydrates (g): 13
          Dietary Fiber (g): 5
          Calories: 111

Food Exchanges: Vegetable: 2½, Fat: 1

Sugar Snap Peas
A hurry-up dish everyone will love. The quick cooking maintains the sweetness and crunchiness of the peas.

2 cups sugar snap peas, washed
3 tablespoons olive oil

Heat the oil in a skillet over medium heat. Add the peas; cover and steam 3 minutes. Remove lid and stir, allowing peas to lightly brown, about 2 minutes.

Serves 4.

1 serving: Total Fat (g): 10
          Protein (g): 3
          Carbohydrates (g): 6
          Dietary Fiber (g): 2
          123 calories

Food Exchanges: Vegetable: ½, Fat: 2

Leeks with Tomatoes

Tasty members of the onion family, leeks are a lovely low glycemic vegetable. Enjoy as much as you like of this side dish without guilt!

6 large leeks (approximately 2 pounds)
2 tablespoons olive oil
1 medium onion, chopped
4 celery stalks
1 (14.5 ounce) can diced tomatoes
1 (4 ounce) can sliced black olives, drained
½ teaspoon salt (to taste)
black pepper (to taste)
¼ - ½ teaspoon oregano

To prepare leeks:

Discard the outer leaves; cut off the root end; cut the top leaves off at the point where the color turns pale. Leeks often have grit inside. I usually slice them in half, and then hold them under running water until the grit is removed.

After cleaning, slice the leeks into 1-inch pieces. Set these aside. Slice the celery into thin slices and set aside, as well.

In a large heavy skillet, heat the olive oil over medium heat. Do not allow the oil to heat to smoking. Add the chopped onion and celery to the heated oil and sauté just until tender and translucent. Add the leeks, tomatoes, olives, and spices (to taste). Stir to combine. Cover with a lid. Reduce the heat to the lowest setting and simmer for about 25 minutes, until the leeks are tender.

Serves 4.

1 serving:	Total Fat (g): 8
	Protein (g): 3
	Total Carbohydrates (g): 23
	Dietary Fiber (g): 4
	192 calories

Food Exchanges: Vegetable: 4½, Fat: 1½

Asparagus Company Casserole

2 pounds fresh asparagus or 2 (1 pound) bags frozen asparagus, thawed
¼ cup heavy cream
¼ cup sour cream
1/3 cup finely grated Parmesan cheese
dash cayenne pepper

Topping
2 tablespoons roasted sunflower kernels
2 tablespoons grated Parmesan cheese

Preheat the oven to 350 degrees. Grease an 8 inch square casserole with butter or non-stick spray. Set aside.

Rinse the asparagus spears, snapping the woody ends from each spear. Discard the ends. If desired, remove the nibs from the sides of each spear with a small paring knife. You can also peel the asparagus, but you will lose some of the volume of the vegetable.

Lay the spears in the casserole, all turned the same way. Set aside.

In a small bowl, mix together the heavy cream, sour cream, 1/3 cup of the Parmesan cheese, and the cayenne pepper. Spoon the mixture evenly over the asparagus. Cover with foil, but leave one edge vented, so that the juices can evaporate. Bake for 30 minutes. Combine the topping ingredients while the asparagus bakes.

Remove the foil after the 30 minutes of baking. Sprinkle the topping evenly over the casserole. Place the dish under the broiler for about 1 minute, just until the topping begins to brown. Remove from the oven and serve.

6 servings.

1 serving: Total Fat (g): 8
Protein (g): 8
Total Carbohydrates (g): 9
Dietary Fiber (g): 4

Food Exchanges: Lean Meat: ½, Vegetable: 1½, Fat: 1½

Asparagus with Hurry-up Sesame Sauce
An easy and elegant dish to whip up for a special dinner. Even though fresh asparagus tastes best, you can further reduce the preparation time by using canned asparagus spears. Just heat them in the microwave while you whip up the sauce!

½ pound fresh asparagus or 2 (10 ounce) packages frozen asparagus
½ teaspoons sesame seeds
1/3 cup mayonnaise (sugar free, if possible)
¼ cup parmesan cheese
¼ teaspoon toasted sesame oil
2 tablespoons heavy cream

Rinse the asparagus spears; then, snap off the woody ends and discard. Remove the scales, if desired, with the sharp edge of a knife or a vegetable peeler. Place the asparagus in a medium skillet and add 2 tablespoons of water. Bring to a quick boil. Cover; then, reduce the heat to the lowest setting and steam about 5 minutes. Remove from heat and arrange the spears on your serving platter or dish.

While the asparagus steams, place the sesame seeds in a small, dry, heavy skillet. Heat the seeds over medium heat about 1 minute, shaking the seeds until they are a golden brown. Immediately remove them from the heat. Add the mayonnaise, cheese, sesame oil and heavy cream to the hot skillet. Do not return to the heat. Stir the sauce quickly with a whisk or a fork. Spoon the sauce over the asparagus to serve.

Serves 5.

1 serving: Total Fat (g): 17
               Protein (g): 4
               Total Carbohydrates (g): 4
               Dietary Fiber (g): 4
               154 calories

Food Exchanges: Lean Meat: ½, Vegetable: ½, Fat: 1½

Spinach Stir-Fry with Bacon Crumbles
A quick side dish, and nice enough for guests.

1 tablespoon olive oil
1 large white onion, sliced into slivers
10 medium asparagus spears, peeled and cut into 1-inch pieces
1 (6 ounce) bag fresh baby spinach, washed, drained, and patted dry
4 slices bacon, cooked, drained and crumbled

Place the oil in a large skillet over medium high heat. Add the onions and briefly cook until the onions are crisp-tender. Add the asparagus and cook, stirring, until onions just begin to brown. Reduce the heat to medium and place the spinach over the vegetables in the skillet. Cover for about 2 minutes, or until the spinach is wilted. Stir over medium heat until the moisture is cooked out, about 1 or 2 minutes. Remove from the heat. Place in a serving dish and garnish with the crumbled bacon.

Serves 4.

1 serving: Total Fat (g): 7
              Protein (g): 4
              Total Carbohydrates (g): 5
              Dietary Fiber (g): 2
              95 calories

Food Exchanges: Lean Meat: ½, Vegetable: 1, Fat: 1

Creamed Spinach
Quick and easy for company or everyday dinners.

3 (10 ounce) packages frozen chopped spinach
¼ cup sour cream
¼ cup cream cheese
½ cup Parmesan cheese, divided
1 slice whole grain bread, torn into crumbs

Cook the spinach according to package directions. Drain in a colander, squeezing out the excess moisture. Mix the spinach, sour cream, cream cheese, and ¼ cup Parmesan cheese. Pour into a small, 1½ quart, greased casserole.

Toss the remaining ¼ cup Parmesan cheese with the breadcrumbs. Sprinkle the cheese and breadcrumbs across the top of the spinach mixture.

Bake 10 to15 minutes at 350 degrees or until hot and the top begins to brown.

Serves 6.

Note: To keep the glycemic values low, do not substitute the sour cream or cheese with reduced fat or fat free products. Always use the real thing!

1 serving: Total Fat (g): 8
Protein (g): 9
Total Carbohydrates (g): 10
Dietary Fiber (g): 5
136 calories

Food Exchanges: Lean Meat: ½, Vegetable: 1½, Fat: 1

Sweet Potato Soufflé
Not just for Thanksgiving

6 large sweet potatoes
1 egg, lightly beaten
¼ cup half & half
2 teaspoons cinnamon
¼ cup unsweetened grated coconut
8 ounces dried cherries
¼ cup blanched, slivered almonds

Pierce the potatoes and microwave according to microwave directions, usually about 4 minutes per potato. (Or, bake 1 hour at 400 degrees) The potatoes are done when they are soft in the center. Pierce each with a knife to check. This can be done a day ahead. If so, refrigerate after cooling.

Preheat the oven to 350 degrees.

Remove the peeling from the potatoes. Combine the sweet potatoes, egg, half & half, and cinnamon in a mixing bowl. Beat until fluffy. Stir in the cherries and coconut.

Place in a greased casserole. Sprinkle with almonds. Bake 30 minutes.

Serve hot or at room temperature.

Serves 10.

1 serving: Total Fat (g): 4
               Protein (g): 3
               Total Carbohydrates (g): 39
               Dietary Fiber (g): 4

Food Exchanges: Starch/Bread: 1½, Fruit: 1, Fat: ½

Sweet Potato Strata
Unusual and tasty

2 cups heavy cream
½ teaspoon nutmeg
¼ teaspoon mace
¼ teaspoon salt
non-stick spray
2 large (or 3 medium) sweet potatoes, peeled and sliced into 3 inch slices
2 large sweet onions, thinly sliced

Combine the cream, nutmeg, mace and salt.

Spray or grease an 8 x 8 inch square casserole. Preheat the oven to 350 degrees.

Layer the onions, covering bottom of casserole. Top with a layer of sweet potatoes, overlapping so that the onions are completely covered. Pour 1/3 of the cream mixture over. Repeat the layers twice more, using the remaining vegetables and cream. Cover loosely with foil, leaving one edge vented. Place in the oven with a foil-lined baking sheet beneath the casserole, as this dish might boil over in the oven.

Bake 1 hour. Remove the foil and bake an additional 30 minutes. The top will be toasty brown.

Let the dish stand 10 to 20 minutes before serving.

Serves 5.

1 serving: Total Fat (g): 22
                Protein (g): 2
                Total Carbohydrates (g): 12
                Dietary Fiber (g): 2
                251 calories

Food Exchanges: Starch/Bread: ½, Vegetable: ½, Fat: 4 ½

Porcupine Patties

4 medium sweet potatoes, cooked and peeled
2 tablespoons butter, melted
1 teaspoon cinnamon
2/3 cup shredded, unsweetened coconut
Non-stick spray

Grease or spray a cookie sheet with non-stick spray. Preheat the oven to 375 degrees.

Place the coconut in the bottom of a small dish. Set aside.

Mash the potatoes. Add the melted butter and cinnamon, mixing well. Form the sweet potatoes into 3-inch patties. Dip each into coconut, coating both sides. Place on a cookie sheet. Spray with non-stick spray. Bake 35 minutes or until the coconut is lightly browned.

Makes about 8 patties.

1 patty: Total Fat (g): 5
            Protein (g): 1
            Total Carbohydrates (g): 17
            Dietary Fiber (g): 3
            Calories: 118

Food Exchanges: Starch/Bread: 1, Fat: 1

French Fried Sweet Potatoes
Who needs white potatoes when you can have these?

1 small sweet potato per person
olive or canola oil
salt

Peel and slice potatoes into ¼-inch to ½-inch fries.

Heat ½ inch oil in the pan until a drop of water sizzles when added. The oil must be hot before the potatoes are added, but never to the point of smoking.

Add the potato slices. Fry approximately 10 minutes, turning once, until the potatoes begin to turn brown. Drain on paper towels. Sprinkle with salt or cinnamon to taste and serve immediately.

1 sweet potato: Total Fat (g): about 14*
Protein (g): 2
Total Carbohydrates (g): 31
Dietary Fiber (g): 4
Calories: about 250*

Food Exchanges: Starch/Bread: 2, Fat: 2½*

* fat varies, according to how well the fries are drained

Green Beans with Almonds

3 tablespoons olive oil
1 small onion, thinly sliced
½ cup slivered or sliced almonds
1 (16 ounce) package frozen French cut green beans
1 cup water

Heat the oil in a large skillet. Add the onions and stir until the onions are translucent. Stir in the almonds and continue to cook over medium heat for about 2 minutes. Stir in the green beans and add water. Cover. Bring to a boil; then reduce the heat to simmer for 30 minutes, stirring occasionally.

Remove the lid and raise the heat to medium-high. Cook and stir until all water is cooked out and the beans have lost their bright green color. The onions will just begin to caramelize when the dish is ready.

Serves 6.

1 serving: Total Fat (g): 13
                  Protein (g): 4
                  Total Carbohydrates (g): 10
                  Dietary Fiber (g): 3
                  162 calories

Food Exchanges: Lean Meat: ½, Vegetable: Fat: 2 ½

Edamame with Green Beans

A pretty side dish with the nutritional benefits of soy beans. If you've been wondering what to do with these healthy green soy beans, here's a tasty recipe to get you started.

1 (16 ounce) package edamame (about 1½ cups shelled)
1 (10 ounce) package frozen green beans
¼ cup diced onion
2 tablespoons olive oil
½ cup water
1 tablespoon sherry
½ teaspoon salt

Rinse edamame pods if you are using unshelled pods. Cover the pods with water in either a microwave-safe bowl or in a pot. Either microwave for 2 minutes or bring to a boil for about a minute on the stove. Drain. Shell the edamame, discarding the outer shells. Set the beans aside.

In a large skillet, heat the olive oil on medium heat and add the onion. Stir briefly until the onion begins to soften. Add the green beans, water, sherry and salt. Cover and cook for about 15 minutes. Add the edamame beans. Cook an additional 5 minutes, until the liquid is gone. Remove to a serving dish and enjoy.

Serves 5.

1 serving: Total Fat (g): 8
                Protein (g): 9
                Total Carbohydrates (g): 13
                Dietary Fiber (g): 6

Food Exchanges: Vegetable: 1, Fat: 1

Green Beans with Mushrooms

3 tablespoons olive oil
1 small onion, cut into thin slivers
8 ounces mushrooms, sliced
½ cup water
1 (16 ounce) bag frozen petite whole green beans
½ teaspoon salt

Heat the oil in a medium sauté pan over medium-high heat. Add the onions and mushrooms. Cook until the onions are translucent.

Remove the lid and raise the heat to high. Quickly cook until the water is gone and the beans begin to sizzle, stirring as needed. Remove immediately from the heat and serve.

Serves 8.

1 serving: Total Fat (g): 5
        Protein (g): 2
        Total Carbohydrates (g): 7
        Dietary Fiber (g): 2
        76 calories

Food Exchanges: Vegetable: 1½, Fat: 1, Other Carb: 0

Southern Style Green Beans
Tender, not crunchy.

1 tablespoon olive oil
½ cup smoked pork chops or ham, diced
1 (16 ounce) bag frozen green beans
½ cup water

In a medium saucepan, heat the oil over medium heat. Add the diced ham and sauté for 2 minutes. Add the beans and the water. Bring to a boil; then reduce the heat to simmer. Cook 20 minutes or more, until the beans are tender, cooking out most of the water.

Serves 5.

1 serving: Total Fat (g): 4
        Protein (g): 4
        Total Carbohydrates (g): 7
        Dietary Fiber (g): 3
        66 calories

Food Exchanges: Lean Meat: ½, Vegetable: 1½, Fat: ½

Spanish Mushrooms
These can be a nice side dish or an appetizer, served in small ramekins.

2 tablespoons olive oil
2 shallots, thinly sliced (about 1½ cups)
1½ pounds mushrooms, preferably mixed varieties, sliced
1 large clove garlic, crushed
¼ teaspoon salt
2 tablespoons red wine

Heat the oil over medium heat. Add the shallots and mushrooms; sauté until shallots are limp, about 10 minutes. Increase the heat to high and continue cooking until the onions and mushrooms begin to brown, about 5 minutes. Add the garlic, wine and salt. Stir quickly over heat 1 additional minute and serve.

Serves 4.

1 serving: Total Fat (g): 7
               Protein (g): 4
               Total Carbohydrates (g): 9
               Dietary Fiber (g): 2
               111 calories

Food Exchanges: Vegetable: 2, Fat: 1½

Brussels Sprouts with Pearl Onions
If you think you don't like Brussels sprouts, try this tasty dish.

1 cup pearl onions
10 ounces fresh Brussels sprouts (about 2½ cups)
4 slices bacon, cooked, drained, and crumbled, reserving the fat
1 tablespoon bacon fat (reserved from the bacon)
Salt and pepper to taste

Drop the pearl onions into boiling water for three minutes. Remove, drain, and rinse in cold water. Cut the root from each onion and press the "pearl" from the onion skin. Trim the tops if necessary. Set aside.

Cut the larger Brussels sprouts in half, remove any dried outer leaves and place the prepared sprouts in a microwave-safe dish. Add ½ cup water. Cover loosely with plastic wrap and microwave on high for 8 minutes.

While the Brussels sprouts are cooking, heat the bacon fat in a large skillet (preferably non-stick). Add the onions to the skillet and cook over medium heat. Stir the onions gently to coat. Continue cooking until the onions are brown on all sides and begin to feel soft. Move the onions to the outside of the pan. Turn off the heat until the Brussels sprouts are ready.

Remove the Brussels sprouts from the microwave. Remove them from the dish with a slotted spoon and place the Brussels sprouts in the skillet with the onions. Over medium heat, gently stir the Brussels sprouts in the fat until they begin to brown, no more than 5 minutes. Gently stir the Brussels sprouts and onions together. Place in a serving dish and top with bacon pieces. Tenderly toss together.

Serves 4.

1 serving: Total Fat (g): 7
               Protein (g): 4
               Total Carbohydrates (g): 8
               Dietary Fiber (g): 3
               105 calories

Food Exchanges: Lean Meat: ½, Vegetable: 1½, Fat: 1

Brussels Sprouts with Caramelized Onions

1 pound Brussels sprouts
1 tablespoon butter or ghee
1 small onion, thinly sliced
2 tablespoons water

Wash Brussels sprouts; cut off the woody ends; remove any dried outer leaves; then, cut each in half. Set aside.

In a medium skillet, heat the butter over medium heat. Add onions and stir to coat. Top with the Brussels sprouts. Add 2 tablespoons water. Cover tightly and steam over very low heat for 12 minutes.

Remove the cover; raise the heat to medium. Continue cooking until the water is gone and the onions become golden brown. Remove to a serving dish and enjoy.

Serves 4.

1 serving: Total Fat (g): 3
　　　　　　Protein (g): 4
　　　　　　Total Carbohydrates (g): 12
　　　　　　Dietary Fiber (g): 4
　　　　　　80 calories

Food Exchanges: Vegetable: 2, Fat: ½

Brussels sprouts

Greek Stir Fry
A marvelous Mediterranean blend of flavors!

1 tablespoon balsamic vinegar
½ teaspoon oregano
1 tablespoon olive oil
1 large red onion, thinly sliced
1 clove garlic, minced
2 (10 ounce) bags fresh spinach
1 (14½ ounce) can diced tomatoes
3 tablespoons feta cheese, crumbled
2 cups hot cooked brown rice

Combine the vinegar and oregano and set aside.

Heat the olive oil on medium heat in a skillet. Add the onion and stir until translucent. Add the garlic; stir, and then add spinach. Cover for 5-10 minutes, until the spinach is wilted.

Remove the cover. Continue cooking until the juices are gone. Add the tomatoes, then the vinegar mixture and toss. Serve over rice (about ½ cup per serving).

Serves 4.

1 serving: Total Fat (g): 7
                 Protein (g): 9
                 Total Carbohydrates (g): 37
                 Dietary Fiber (g): 7
                 228 calories

Food Exchanges: Starch/Bread: 1½, Vegetable: 2½, Fat: 1

Asian Stir Fry
Buy everything pre-cut for a hurry-up side dish.

2 tablespoons sesame oil, divided
½ cup onion, cut into thick slivers
1 cup sliced mushrooms
1 clove garlic, finely minced
2 cups broccoli flowerettes
1 teaspoon fresh ginger, grated
1 tablespoon soy sauce
1 tablespoon sherry

Heat 1 tablespoon oil in a wok or skillet. Add the onion and mushrooms. Cook over medium-high heat for about 5 minutes, until the onions are tender and moisture is nearly cooked out. Add the garlic. Stir.

Quickly add the broccoli and ginger. Continue to stir until the broccoli is crisp-tender, about 3 minutes. Add the soy sauce and sherry. Stir to mix. Continue cooking until all liquid is gone, just another minute or two. Remove from the heat, stir in the sesame oil, and serve hot.

Serves 4.

1 serving: Total Fat (g): 7
             Protein (g): 2
             Total Carbohydrates (g): 5
             Dietary Fiber (g): 2
             92 calories

Food Exchanges: Vegetable: 1, Fat: 1½

Broccoli with Pasta Shells

1 ½ cups whole wheat or spelt pasta shells
½ pound broccoli flowerettes
2 cups half & half
8 ounces fresh mushrooms, sliced
¼ cup butter
1/8 teaspoon pepper
1 cup grated Parmesan cheese

Cook the pasta shells in boiling water, according to package directions.

Meanwhile, rinse the broccoli, place in a microwave safe dish, cover with plastic wrap, leaving one edge open to vent. Microwave for 3 minutes. Remove.

Drain the shells when done and return to the empty pot. Add all the ingredients but the cheese. Heat over low heat for 2 minutes or until the butter is melted. Toss in the cheese and serve.

Serves 6.

1 serving: Total Fat (g): 22
                Protein (g): 14
                Total Carbohydrates (g): 27
                Dietary Fiber (g): 4
                345 calories

Food Exchanges: Starch/Bread: 1½, Lean Meat: 1, Vegetable: ½, Fat: 4

Penne Pasta with Broccoli

2 cups chopped broccoli
2 cups cooked whole grain penne pasta, drained
2 medium tomatoes, diced with seeded pulp removed
¼ cup extra virgin olive oil
1 clove garlic, crushed
¼ teaspoon crushed red pepper
¼ teaspoon salt

Place the chopped broccoli in a microwave safe dish. Loosely cover with plastic wrap and microwave for 2 minutes. Set aside.

In a medium saucepan, heat the oil over medium heat. Stir in the garlic, pepper and salt. Gently toss in the pasta, broccoli and tomatoes. Remove from heat and serve.

Serves 6.

1 serving: Total Fat (g): 9
            Protein (g): 4
            Total Carbohydrates (g): 16
            Dietary Fiber (g): 3
            155 calories

Food Exchanges: Starch/Bread: 1, Vegetable: ½, Fat: 2

Glazed Acorn Squash

2 acorn squash
2 tablespoons butter, melted
3 tablespoons fructose (or ¼ cup alternative granulated sweetener)
1 teaspoon cinnamon
1/8 teaspoon ground cardamon
2 teaspoons lemon juice

Wash and slice the squash ¾ inch thick, removing the seeds.

Mix the fructose and spices together. Set aside.

Pour ¼ cup water into a large, greased casserole dish. Arrange the squash in a casserole dish. Brush the squash slices with butter. Sprinkle with the fructose and spice mixture.

Cover and bake at 350 degrees for 30 to 40 minutes or until tender.

Serves 4.

1 serving: Total Fat (g): 6
Protein (g): 2
Total Carbohydrates (g): 37 (with fructose)
Dietary Fiber (g): 4
192 calories

Food Exchanges: Starch/Bread: 1½, Fat: 1, Other Carb: 1

Butternut Squash with Tarragon
A sophisticated side dish

1 medium butternut squash
1 tablespoon butter
1 teaspoon dried tarragon
½ teaspoon salt
2 tablespoons cooking sherry

Preheat the oven to 400 degrees.

Wash the squash with water. Pat dry with a paper towel. Slice in half lengthwise. Spray the squash with non-stick spray or lightly oil the skin. Place the squash, cut-side-up, in a baking dish. Cover loosely with foil.

Bake 45 minutes to 1 hour, until there is no resistance when knife is inserted in the thickest part (or follow directions for your microwave, covering with plastic wrap instead of foil and leaving an edge open to vent). Cool 5 minutes.

Scoop the pulp of the squash from the peeling and place in a medium bowl. Add the remaining ingredients. Stir with a spoon or wire whip until smooth. Serve hot.

Serves 5.

1 serving: Total Fat (g): 3
        Protein (g): 4
        Total Carbohydrates (g): 40
        Dietary Fiber (g): 6
        183 calories

Food Exchanges: Starch/Bread: 2½, Fat: ½

Mashed Butternut Squash
Better than mashed potatoes!

1 medium butternut squash
½ teaspoon salt
1/8 teaspoon black pepper
1 tablespoon butter

Preheat the oven to 400 degrees.

Split the squash in half, lengthwise and remove the seeds with the edge of a spoon. Spray with non-stick spray and place in a casserole dish, cut-side-up. Cover loosely with foil. Bake for 45 minutes, until there is no resistance when a knife is inserted in the thickest part. (If you're in a hurry, cover dish with plastic wrap, leaving one edge open to vent. Microwave on high, following manufacturer's cooking times, until tender.)

Scoop the pulp of the squash from the peeling and place in a medium bowl. Add the salt, pepper, and butter. Stir with a spoon or wire whip until smooth. Serve hot.

Serves 5.

1 serving: Total Fat (g): 3
            Protein (g): 4
            Total Carbohydrates (g): 40
            Dietary Fiber (g): 6
            174 calories

Food Exchanges: Starch/Bread: 2½, Fat: ½

Zucchini with Ginger

This spicy recipe is made with fresh ginger and adds an Asian flavor to your meal. Try serving it with ham or pork for a delicious side dish.

2 pounds small zucchini
1 medium apple
2 tablespoons olive oil
2 tablespoons soy sauce
2 tablespoons toasted sesame oil
1 tablespoon Worcestershire sauce
1 teaspoon fructose or agave syrup (or 1½ teaspoon alternative granular sweetener)
1 clove garlic
½ teaspoon dried red pepper flakes
about 1 inch of unpeeled, fresh ginger root
1 green spring onion

Wash and trim the ends from the zucchini. Slice the squash into ¼ inch slices and set aside.

Peel and core the apple. Cut the apple into thin, ¼ inch slices.

Heat the olive oil in a large skillet over medium high heat. When the skillet is hot enough for a drop of water to sizzle in the pan, add the zucchini and the apple slices and reduce the heat to medium. Sauté the apple and zucchini together for about 5 minutes, stirring as needed. Set aside, covered.

While the apple and zucchini are cooking:
In a medium bowl, combine the soy sauce, toasted sesame oil, Worchestershire sauce, sweetener and pepper flakes.

Grate the ginger and add to the sesame oil mixture. Trim and thinly slice the spring onion and add to the bowl.

Add the cooked zucchini and apples to the dressing mixture and gently toss all together to evenly mix. May be served hot or at room temperature.

Serves 6.

1 serving: Total Fat (g): 9
              Protein (g): 2
              Total Carbohydrates (g): 9
              Dietary Fiber (g): 2
              122 calories

Food Exchanges: Vegetable: 1, Fat: 2

Wild Rice with Mushrooms
A great buffet dish when doubled.

1 tablespoon butter
½ cup mushrooms, sliced
½ cup green onions, sliced1 clove garlic, minced
1 (14½ ounces) can beef broth
2/3 cup wild rice, rinsed thoroughly
¼ teaspoon salt
1/8 teaspoon black pepper

In a medium saucepan, melt the butter. Add the mushrooms, onions, and garlic. Sauté about 1 minute. Add the broth and bring to a boil. Stir in the rice, salt, and pepper. Cover tightly. Cook 55 to 60 minutes, until tender. Pour off the excess liquid, if any.

Serves 6.

1 serving: Total Fat (g): 2
                   Protein (g): 7
                   Total Carbohydrates (g): 21
                   Dietary Fiber (g): 3
                   127 calories

Food Exchanges: Starch/Bread: 1, Lean Meat: ½, Vegetable: 1½, Fat: ½

Spanish Rice
Delicious with a Mexican meal.

3 teaspoons olive oil
1 cup brown rice (long cooking)
¾ cup chopped onion
½ cup chopped celery
¼ cup diced green pepper (optional)
1 can (14 to16 ounces) diced tomatoes
1¼ cup water
1½ teaspoon salt
2 teaspoons chili powder

In a saucepan, sauté the onion, celery, green pepper and rice in the olive oil until the onion is translucent and tender. Add the water and remaining ingredients. Bring to a boil. Cover tightly and simmer 45 to 50 minutes, until all the liquid is absorbed.

Serves 6.

1 serving: Total Fat (g): 4
                   Protein (g): 3
                   Total Carbohydrates (g): 30
                   Dietary Fiber (g): 2
                   162 calories

Food Exchanges: Starch/Bread: ½, Vegetable: 1, Fat: ½

Basic Rice Pilaf

1 tablespoon butter
½ cup onion, chopped
½ cup brown rice
2 cloves garlic, minced
½ cup wild rice
1 (16 ounce) can chicken broth*

Rinse the rice if directed on the package. Melt the butter in a medium pot. Add the onion and rice; sauté on medium high, until the onion is translucent. The bottom of the pan will begin to brown. Add the garlic. Stir.

Immediately add the chicken broth. Bring to a boil. Reduce the heat to low and simmer, covered, for 50 minutes or until rice is tender and water is absorbed.

*Beef broth may be substituted for a heartier flavor or to enhance a red meat entree.

Serves 4.

1 serving: Total Fat (g): 4
         Protein (g): 7
         Total Carbohydrates (g): 36
         Dietary Fiber (g): 2
         211 calories

Food Exchanges: Starch/Bread: 2, Vegetable: ½, Fat: 1

Coconut Rice
Creamy rice with a taste of Thailand.

1 (14 ounce) can lite coconut milk
1 cup water
1 cup whole grain brown rice (long cooking)

Rinsse the brown rice if directed on the package. Bring the coconut milk and water to boil in a medium saucepan. Rinse the rice, if directed on package. Add the rice to the saucepan and cover tightly. Simmer 45 to 55 minutes over low heat until the moisture is mostly absorbed and the rice is tender.

Serves 6.

1 serving: Total Fat (g): 4
         Protein (g): 3
         Total Carbohydrates (g): 27
         Dietary Fiber (g): 2
         153 calories

Food Exchanges: Starch/Bread: 1½, Fat: 1

Creamy Rice with Broccoli

1 cup brown rice (long cooking)
1 tablespoon olive oil
1 small onion, diced (about 3 cup)
½ teaspoon salt
2 cups water
1 cup broccoli, chopped
¼ cup Romano cheese
¼ cup light cream

Rinse the rice if directed on the package. Sauté the onion with the oil in a medium saucepan. Add the rice, salt and water; bring to a boil. Cover and cook over low heat for 45 minutes.

Stir in the broccoli, cheese, and cream. Cover and cook an additional 5 to 10 minutes or until all the liquid is absorbed.

Serves 6.

1 serving: Total Fat (g): 6
                 Protein (g): 5
                 Total Carbohydrates (g): 27
                 Dietary Fiber (g): 1
                 183 calories

Food Exchanges: Starch/Bread: 1½, Vegetable: ½, Fat: 1

Arroz Verde
South of the Border

3 teaspoons olive oil
1 cup brown rice
¾ cup onion, minced
1 cup fresh cilantro, loosely packed in measuring cup
3 garlic cloves, crushed
1 small can (4 ounce) peeled jalapeno peppers, cut into chunks
1 can chicken broth plus enough water to equal 2 cups
½ teaspoon salt
Sour cream (optional)

Sauté the rice and onion in oil until the onion is translucent. Remove from the heat.

Place the cilantro, garlic, peppers, and chicken bullion in a blender or food processor. Puree.

Pour into the pot with the rice. (If you desire a more delicate flavor, strain the cilantro mixture and press as much liquid as possible into the rice. The resulting rice will not be as green, but will have much of the flavor.) Add the salt and stir.

Bring to a boil. Cover and simmer 50 minutes or until the liquid is absorbed and the rice is tender.

Garnish with sour cream, if desired.

Serves 6.

1 serving: Total Fat (g): 4
Protein (g): 5
Total Carbohydrates (g): 28
Dietary Fiber (g): 2
162 calories

Food Exchanges: Starch/Bread: 1½, Vegetable: ½, Fat: ½

Baked Beans

4 thick slices sugar-free bacon (or 8 thin slices)
1 small onion, minced
2 (15 ounce) cans navy beans, drained
1 (8 ounce) can tomato puree
3 tablespoons fructose
1 tablespoon vinegar
1 tablespoon dry mustard
¼ teaspoon allspice
¼ teaspoon cayenne pepper
1 tablespoon Worcestershire sauce

Cook the bacon until crisp. Reserve 1 teaspoon bacon fat. Drain and crumble the bacon. Set aside.

Put 1 teaspoon bacon fat in a skillet and heat over medium-high. Add the onions and cook until the onions are translucent and begin to brown. Reduce the heat to medium; stir in the remaining ingredients except the bacon crumbles.

Pour into a greased casserole. Top with the crumbled bacon.

Bake at 350 degrees for 15 to 45 minutes. The longer time allows the beans to absorb more of the sauce.

Serves 8.

1 serving: Total Fat (g): 4
                Protein (g): 11
                Total Carbohydrates (g): 33
                Dietary Fiber (g): 6
                203 calories

Food Exchanges: Starch/Bread: 1½, Lean Meat: ½, Vegetable: ½, Fat: ½, Other Carb: ½

Cookies & Bars

Apricot Swirls

1 (12 ounce) package dried apricots*
1 cup pecan pieces
½ cup half & half
1½ cups kamut flour (whole wheat or spelt flour may be used)
½ cup oat bran
1 teaspoon cinnamon
¼ cup fructose or agave syrup (or 1/3 cup Splenda or alternative sweetener)
½ teaspoon salt
1½ teaspoons baking powder
½ cup butter, melted
2 eggs
waxed paper

To make the filling:
Place the apricots, pecans, and half & half in a food processor. Process until coarsely chopped. Set aside.

Mix together the dry ingredients. Set aside.

To make the dough:
In a medium bowl, whisk the butter and fructose together. Beat in the eggs. With a large spoon, add the dry ingredients.

Lay about 18 inches of waxed paper on a damp surface and press down, pressing out air bubbles. This will be your working surface.

Sprinkle the waxed paper with a small amount of flour. Place the dough on top; press down; sprinkle flour on the dough. Roll the dough into a rectangle, about 11 x 16 inches. Spread the filling evenly over the dough, and then press the filling into the dough.

Using the waxed paper and starting with the long edge of the dough, roll the dough lengthwise, pulling the paper away as you roll. Press the long edge into the length of dough when finished. Wrap the rolled dough in waxed paper and refrigerate for 2 or more hours.

Open the waxed paper and slice cookies into ½ inch slices. Place on a lightly greased cookie sheet. Bake at 350 degrees for 12 minutes, until lightly browned. Store in an airtight container.

Makes 3 dozen cookies.

1 bar: Total Fat (g): 5
Protein (g): 2
Total Carbohydrates (g): 14 (with fructose or agave syrup)
Dietary Fiber (g): 2
101 calories

Food Exchanges: Starch/Bread: 1½, Fruit: ½, Fat: 1

*Dried figs may be substituted.

Apricot Bars

Filling
1 (12 ounce) package dried apricots, sliced*
1 (12 ounce) can crushed pineapple in its own juice
1/3 cup Splenda (or alternative granular sweetener)

Dough
1½ cups whole-wheat flour
½ cup unsweetened coconut
1 cup oatmeal
¼ cup oat bran
½ teaspoon salt
½ teaspoon baking soda
1 teaspoon cinnamon
¼ cup canola oil
¼ cup butter, melted
3 eggs, beaten

Combine all the filling ingredients in a small saucepan. Cook and stir over medium-low heat until thickened and pasty, about 30 minutes.

Preheat the oven to 350 degrees.

To make the dough, combine the flour, coconut, oatmeal, oat bran, salt, baking soda and salt. Add the oil, melted butter and eggs. Stir until mixed.

Spray a rectangular casserole dish with non-stick spray. Pat half of the dough into an even layer in the dish. Top with apricot mixture and spread evenly. Put the remainder of the dough on top, dropping by spoonfuls. Pat the pieces of dough together into an even layer, covering all of the apricot mixture. Bake for 35 to 40 minutes, until brown.

*Figs may be substituted for apricots.

Makes 28 bars.

1 bar: Total Fat (g): 5
        Protein (g): 3
        Total Carbohydrates (g): 17
        Dietary Fiber (g): 3
        115 calories

Food Exchanges: Starch/Bread: ½, Fruit: ½, Fat: 1

Cream Cheese Nut Bars

¼ cup melted butter
2 tablespoons softened butter
3 eggs
½ cup Splenda (or alternative granular sweetener)
2 tablespoons fructose
1½ teaspoon vanilla, divided
½ cup + 1 tablespoon whole wheat flour*
¾ teaspoon baking powder
¼ teaspoon salt
1 cup nuts, coarsely chopped
1 (3 ounce package) cream cheese, softened

Preheat the oven to 350 degrees. Melt ¼ cup butter. Set aside.

Beat 2 eggs in a medium bowl. Gradually add the Splenda. Beat until thick and lemon colored. Add the melted butter and 1 teaspoon vanilla. Stir. Set aside.

Mix ½ cup flour, baking powder, and salt in a small bowl. Gradually add to the egg mixture, stirring well. Stir in the nuts. Pour the batter into a well-greased 9-inch square pan.

Cream the remaining 2 tablespoons butter and cream cheese. Gradually add the fructose. Beat until light and fluffy. Add 1 egg; beat well. Add the remaining flour (1 tablespoon) and vanilla (½ teaspoon). Stir well. Pour evenly over the batter in the pan.

Bake 30 minutes or until a toothpick inserted in the center comes out clean. Cool completely in the pan. Cut into 1½ inch squares.

Makes about 3 dozen.

1 bar: Total Fat (g): 5
        Protein (g): 1
        Total Carbohydrates (g): 4
        Dietary Fiber (g): 1
        68 calories

Food Exchanges: Fat: 1

*Spelt or kamut flour may be substituted.

Spicy Pumpkin Bars

½ cup + 2 tablespoons whole wheat flour
¼ cup defatted soy flour
1 tablespoon flaxseed meal (optional)
½ teaspoon ground allspice
½ teaspoon cinnamon
¼ teaspoon ground ginger
1 teaspoon baking powder
¼ teaspoon salt
4 eggs, divided
3/4 cup Splenda (or alternative granular sweetener)
2 tablespoons agave or fructose
1 (15 ounce) can pumpkin
¼ cup melted butter + 3 tablespoons softened butter, divided
1½ teaspoons vanilla, divided
1 (8 ounce) package cream cheese, softened
1 cup nuts, coarsely chopped

Preheat the oven to 325 degrees. Spray or grease a 9x13 inch-baking dish.

In a medium mixing bowl, combine the dry ingredients: ½ cup whole-wheat flour, soy flour, flaxseed meal, spices, baking powder and salt. Set aside.

Beat 3 eggs in a large mixing bowl. Gradually add the ¾ cup Splenda, beating. Add the pumpkin and ¼ cup melted butter and mix well. Stir in 1 teaspoon vanilla. Stir the dry ingredients into the pumpkin mixture. Add the nuts and mix with spoon. Pour into the baking dish.

In a small bowl, combine the cream cheese, 1 egg, 3 tablespoons softened butter, 2 tablespoons remaining sweetener, ½ teaspoon vanilla, and 2 tablespoons flour. Spread evenly over the pumpkin mixture. Bake 35 to 40 minutes. Mixture will be lightly brown when done.

Makes 24 bars.

1 bar with Splenda and fructose or agave: Total Fat (g): 11
Protein (g): 4
Total Carbohydrates (g): 7
Dietary Fiber (g): 1
125 calories

Food Exchanges: Starch/Bread: ½, Lean Meat: ½, Fat: 2

Fig Bars

Filling
2 (8 ounce) packages dried figs
2 cups water
¼ cup fructose or agave syrup
½ teaspoon cinnamon

Crust
1 cup whole-wheat flour
½ cup unsweetened coconut, grated
½ cup oat bran
½ teaspoon salt
½ teaspoon baking soda
¼ cup Splenda (or granular alternative sweetener)
1 teaspoon cinnamon
6 tablespoons butter, softened
1 egg, beaten with 2 tablespoons water

In a medium saucepan, place all the filling ingredients and simmer over low heat. Cook for about 3 hours, until the figs are tender and the consistency of paste. Add water during cooking as needed. Cool; process in a food processor or blender. The filling may be made up to two weeks ahead. Store in a refrigerator until ready to use.

To make the crust, combine the dry ingredients. Add the softened butter with a pastry blender or fork. The dough should be crumbly. Pour the egg mixture into the center of the dough and mix with a fork until the dough holds together. Divide the dough into two halves. Spray an 8-inch square pan with non-stick spray. Press half of dough evenly into the bottom of the pan. Spread the fig mixture evenly. Crumble the remaining dough over the top, and then pat together so that the figs are covered.

Bake at 350 degrees for 30 to 35, until the top is lightly browned. Slice into squares while hot; then cool before removing from the pan.

Makes 16 (2-inch) bars.

1 bar: Total Fat (g): 6
        Protein (g): 3
        Total Carbohydrates (g): 31
        Dietary Fiber (g): 5
        173 calories

Food Exchanges: Starch/Bread: ½, Fruit: 1, Fat: 1, Other Carb: ½

Chocolate Chunk Cookies

2 fructose-sweetened Dark Chocolate Bars (2.8 ounces) or Lindt 70% cocoa bars
½ cup pecans or walnuts, chopped
½ cup butter, softened
2/3 cup fructose or agave syrup
1 egg
½ teaspoon vanilla
1 cup whole wheat flour*
¾ teaspoon baking soda
½ teaspoon salt

Preheat the oven to 375 degrees.

Break the chocolate bars into squares. Chop each square into quarters or irregular chunks with a sharp knife on a cutting board. Add the nuts. Set aside.

In a medium mixing bowl, cream the butter. Gradually add the fructose. Add the egg and vanilla, mixing well.

In a separate bowl, mix together the flour, soda, salt and the chocolate/nut mixture, stirring with a large spoon. Add to the creamed mixture.

Using a teaspoon, drop the cookie dough onto an ungreased cookie sheet. Bake 8 minutes. Let cool slightly before removing from the cookie sheet. Remove and complete cooling the cookies on a wire rack or flat surface.

Makes 3 dozen.

*Spelt or kamut flour may be substituted.

2 cookies: Total Fat (g): 11
Protein (g): 2
Total Carbohydrates (g): 22
Dietary Fiber (g): 1

Food Exchanges: Starch/Bread: ½, Fat: 1½, Other Carb: ½

Scottish Shortbread Fans
Cardamom adds a wonderful fragrance and authentic flavor.

1 cup unsalted butter, softened
2/3 cup fructose or agave syrup
2 cups whole grain pastry flour
¼ teaspoon ground cardamom
¼ teaspoon salt

Spray 2 cookie sheets with non-stick cooking spray. Preheat the oven to 300 degrees.

Cream the butter in a medium mixing bowl. Gradually add the fructose, beating until light and fluffy. Add the flour, cardamom, and salt; stir until well blended.

Divide the dough into 4 equal portions. Form each into a ball. Pat into 5-inch circles, 2 per cookie sheet.

Score the surface of each circle into eight wedges, using a wooden toothpick. Then, using a fork, press the tines into the outside edges of each circle.

Bake 30 minutes or until the cookies are lightly browned. Cool completely. Break into wedges to serve.

Store in an airtight container.

Makes 32 cookie wedges.

2 cookies: Total Fat (g): 10
Protein (g): 2
Total Carbohydrates (g): 21
Dietary Fiber (g): 2
176 calories

Food Exchanges: Starch/Bread: ½, Fat: 2, Other Carb: ½

Cinnamon Walnut Cookies
Enjoy these tasty bites without guilt!

2 cups walnuts
1 cup whole grain pastry flour
½ cup low fat or defatted soy flour
½ cup oat bran
1 teaspoon ground cinnamon
¼ teaspoon salt
1 cup butter, softened
2/3 cup fructose or Whey Low D granules (or ¾ cup Splenda)

Preheat the oven to 300 degrees.

Place the walnuts, flours, bran, cinnamon and salt in a food processor using the sharp blade. Briefly process the mixture, just until the nuts are finely chopped and evenly mixed. Set aside.

In a medium bowl, cream the softened butter. Add the sweetener and beat until fluffy. Beat in the egg until thoroughly mixed. Add the dry ingredients to the butter mixture and stir until evenly mixed.

If desired, line your baking sheets with parchment paper. Otherwise, use ungreased baking sheets. Taking walnut-sized pieces of the batter, roll the cookie mixture into 1-inch diameter balls and place each on the baking sheet, placing them about 2 inches apart. Using a fork, gently press each cookie to about ¼ inch thickness. Drag the tines of the fork across, leaving lines in each cookie.

Bake 15 minutes. The cookies will be lightly browned. Cool a few minutes, then gently slide a spatula beneath each to loosen. Move to a rack or flat surface to finish cooling. If you used the parchment, just slide the whole thing onto your countertop after loosening.

Makes 5 dozen cookies.

1 cookie: Total Fat (g): 6
Protein (g): 2
Total Carbohydrates (g): 5
Dietary Fiber (g): 1
76 calories

Food Exchanges: Lean Meat: ¼, Fat: 1

If you cook more than one sheet of cookies at a time, be sure to stagger the sheets in the oven, never placing one directly over the other. Leave space at the edges of the sheets rather than placing them all the way to the wall of the oven, so that the heat can circulate properly.

Shake Off the Sugar Cookies

Packed with protein and delicately spiced with nutmeg, these cookies are a safe and tasty bite of sweetness. Try these low-glycemic cookies for a treat any time.

Cookies
½ cup low carb or soy baking mix
1 cup whole grain pastry flour
½ teaspoon baking soda
¼ teaspoon ground nutmeg
½ cup butter, softened
1 egg
1/3 cup Splenda
2 tablespoons agave (or fructose or Whey Low)
2 tablespoons heavy cream
½ teaspoon vanilla
3-inch cookie cutters

Sugar Glaze
1 cup *Whey Low powder
1½ -2 tablespoons heavy cream
½ teaspoon vanilla
food coloring (paste coloring or Dec-a-Cake brand work well)
about 1 tablespoon cocoa

To make the cookies:
In a medium bowl, mix together the baking mix, flour, baking soda and nutmeg. Using a pastry blender cut in the butter until the mixture is in pea-sized particles. This may be done in a food processor, as well, or with a fork. Set aside.

In a small bowl, beat the egg. Add the sweeteners, vanilla and cream. Add to the dry mixture, stirring until well blended. Form into a ball, cover, and refrigerate for at least an hour.

When you are ready to roll the cookies, preheat the oven to 350 degrees.

Lightly flour your surface for rolling the cookies. Place the cold dough on the surface; lightly dust the top of the dough with flour. With your rolling pin, roll the dough to about 1/8 inch thick. Cut with cookie cutter and place on an ungreased cookie sheet. First lining the cookie sheet with parchment makes the process easier, but is not essential. Gather up the leftover remnants of dough, then re-roll and cut them, as well. Place these on the cookie sheet along with the others. If necessary, bake the cookies on two sheets. If you do put 2 cookie sheets in the oven, stagger them, so that one is not directly over the other. This allows for more even browning.

Bake about 5 minutes. Remove. Cool slightly, then glaze if desired.

To make sugar glaze:
Place the Whey Low powder in a small bowl. Add cream and vanilla to a nice spreading

consistency. Add food colors as desired, dividing the glaze if you need more than one color. Ice the cookies while still a bit warm, reserving a few tablespoons of glaze for adding features, if desired.

Add the cocoa to the reserved glaze. Place in a pastry bag and pipe on the eyes and mouth. This works nicely for "ghost" and "jack-o-lantern" cookies. Let dry and enjoy!

Makes 12 big (3-inch diameter) cookies.

*Whey Low Powder is available at www.wheylow.com.

1 cookie, without icing: Total Fat (g): 9
Protein (g): 5
Total Carbohydrates (g): 9
Dietary Fiber (g): 1
143 calories

Food Exchanges: Starch/Bread: ½, Fat: 2

1 cookie, with icing: Total Fat (g): 10
Protein (g): 5
Total Carbohydrates (g): 25
Dietary Fiber (g): 1
240 calories (assuming Whey D is equal in calories to fructose)

Food Exchanges: Starch/Bread: ½, Fat: 2, Other Carb: 2

Choco-Cherry Squares
Dense, moist, and packed with protein

1/3 cup whole-wheat pastry flour
¼ cup soy flour
2/3 cup fructose or agave syrup
5 eggs
4 squares unsweetened chocolate
½ cup butter
1 tablespoon walnuts, chopped
1 tablespoon vanilla extract
8 ounces softened cream cheese
about ½ cup black cherry all-fruit preserves

Grease or spray an 8 x 12 inch baking dish. Preheat oven to 300 degrees.

Combine the whole wheat and soy flours. Set aside.

Melt the chocolate and butter together according to directions on the chocolate package, usually about 1 minute in microwave. Stir together when melted.

Beat the eggs and fructose together with a whisk.

With a whisk or large spoon, beat the dry ingredients into the egg mixture. Beat in the chocolate/butter mixture, adding slowly. Mix in the walnuts and vanilla. Pour into the greased baking dish.

Bake 30 to 35 minutes until the center tests done.

Cool completely. Cut into 2 inch squares. Spread each square with cream cheese. Top with a small dollop of cherry preserves. Store in the refrigerator. Let stand at room temperature about 30 minutes before serving.

Makes 24 (2 inch) squares.

1 bar: Total Fat (g): 11
              Protein (g): 3
              Total Carbohydrates (g): 15
              Dietary Fiber (g): 1

Food Exchanges: Lean Meat: ½, Fat: 2, Other Carb: ½

Coconut Macaroons
So easy.

2 egg whites*
2/3 cup fructose (granular sweetener like maltitol may be used – Splenda may not work as well)
1 teaspoon vanilla
dash salt
1½ cups unsweetened coconut

Lightly grease 2 cookie sheets. Preheat the oven to 300 degrees.

Beat the egg whites in a ceramic or metal bowl until foamy. Gradually add the sweetener and continue beating until the whites are stiff, but not dry. Stir in the vanilla and dash of salt.

Fold in the coconut.

Drop by teaspoonfuls onto the cookie sheets. Bake for 15 minutes, until they just begin to brown.

Cool about 5 minutes, then gently remove the macaroons from the cookie sheets with a flat spatula. Cool completely on wire racks. Store in an airtight container.

Makes 3 dozen.

2 cookies: Total Fat (g): 2
           Protein (g): 1
           Total Carbohydrates (g): 12(fructose), 1 (maltitol)
           Dietary Fiber (g): 2
           Calories: 66 (fructose), 26 (maltitol)

Food Exchanges: Fat: ½, Other Carb: ½ (fructose)

Just Whites powdered egg whites are nice to keep on hand when you only need the whites. They work just as well as the fresh egg whites. Just follow the directions on the can to reconstitute

Macadamia Nut Cookies
Very nice, a cake-like cookie that's perfect for tea.

2 cups whole-wheat pastry flour
¾ cup oat bran
2 teaspoons baking powder
½ teaspoon salt
¾ cup butter
¼ cup fructose or agave syrup
¼ cup Splenda
2 eggs
1 teaspoon vanilla
1 cup macadamia nuts, chopped into large pieces

Preheat the oven to 350 degrees. Grease the baking sheets.
Mix the dry ingredients and set aside.

Cream the butter and sugar together. Beat in the eggs, mixing well. Add the vanilla. Mix in the dry ingredients and nuts until well combined. Drop by teaspoonfuls onto a greased baking sheet.

Bake 9 to 10 minutes or until the edges begin to brown.

Cool about 2 minutes on cookie sheet. Remove and finish cooling on a rack or waxed paper.

Makes 3½ dozen.

1 cookie: Total Fat (g): 6
Protein (g): 1
Total Carbohydrates (g): 8
Dietary Fiber (g): 1
82 calories

Food Exchanges: Starch/Bread: ½, Fat: 1

Spelt Brownies

1cup fructose or agave syrup
½ cup Splenda (or alternative granular sweetener)
1 cup spelt flour*
1 cup defatted soy flour
2 teaspoons baking powder
½ teaspoon salt
1 cup butter
4 squares unsweetened chocolate
4 eggs, beaten
¾ cup applesauce
2 teaspoons vanilla extract
2 cups pecans or walnuts, chopped, if desired

Preheat the oven to 325 degrees. Grease a 13 x 9 x 2 inch-baking dish.

Combine the flours, fructose, Splenda, baking powder, and salt. If using agave, combine it with the butter and chocolate. Set aside.

Combine the butter and chocolate. Microwave on high 2 minutes. Stir. Microwave an additional 30 seconds, if the chocolate is not yet melted. Stir until melted. Place in a large bowl.

Slowly whisk the eggs into the chocolate mixture. If the mixture is very hot, first whisk a small amount of the chocolate mixture into eggs, then add the egg mixture to chocolate. Whisk in the applesauce.

Add the dry ingredients to the chocolate mixture. Stir in the vanilla and nuts.

Pour into the greased baking dish. Bake for 25 minutes. Cool and cut into 2-inch squares. Store in an airtight container.

Yield: 2 dozen brownies

*Whole wheat or kamut flour may be substituted.

1 brownie: Total Fat (g): 17
             Protein (g): 4
             Total Carbohydrates (g): 21
             Dietary Fiber (g): 3
             240 calories

Food Exchanges: Starch/Bread: ½, Lean Meat: ½, Fat: 3½, Other Carb: 1

Dessert

Chocolate Hazelnut Cheesecake
Heavenly!

Coconut Pastry Crust
1 cup whole-wheat flour
1 ¼ cups unsweetened coconut
1/3 cup butter, melted
1 tablespoon cold water

Cheesecake
¾ cup fructose (alternative granular sweetener may be used)
½ cup cocoa
3 (8 ounce) packages cream cheese
1 cup sour cream
5 eggs
1 (8 ounce) package chopped hazelnuts, divided
2 teaspoons vanilla

To make the crust:
Combine the flour, coconut, and melted butter in a medium bowl. Mix in the water with a fork. Press into the bottom and halfway up the sides of a 9-inch springform pan. Run your finger around the top edge, gently pressing the crust so that the top edge is even and smooth.

Preheat the oven to 350 degrees.

To make the cheesecake:
Mix the fructose and cocoa together in a small bowl. Set aside.

Puree 1 cup of the hazelnuts. Set aside the remaining chopped nuts for topping.

In a large mixing bowl, beat the cream cheese with the sour cream until creamy. Add the eggs, beating well. Beat in the fructose mixture, then the pureed hazelnuts and vanilla. Pour into the prepared pan. Sprinkle the reserved chopped hazelnuts evenly over the top and gently press the nuts onto the batter, but leaving the nuts exposed.

Bake at 1 hour. When done, a knife inserted near the center should come out clean. Remove and cool for 15 minutes. Remove the sides of the springform pan and cool completely. If desired, top with fructose sweetened whipping cream.

Store in refrigerator.

Serves 12.

1 slice: Total Fat (g): 40
Protein (g): 11
Total Carbohydrates (g): 33 (fructose), 15 (alternative sweetener)
Dietary Fiber (g): 4
Calories 508 (fructose), 440 (alternative sweetener)

Food Exchanges: Starch/Bread: ½, Lean Meat: 1, Fat: 7½, Other Carb: 1

Pecan Praline Cheesecake

Crust
1 cup pecan pieces
½ cup oat bran
½ cup whole grain pastry flour
1/3 cup softened butter
2 tablespoon cold water

Cheesecake
½ cup pecan halves
2 tablespoons butter
3 (8 ounces) packages cream cheese
1 cup sour cream
4 eggs
¾ cup + 1 teaspoon fructose, divided (alternative sweetener may be substituted)
1 teaspoon vanilla
1½ teaspoon maple flavoring

To make the crust:
Preheat the oven to 400 degrees. Place the pecan pieces, oat bran, pastry flour, and butter in processor. Blend with the knife attachment. When mixed, add the water while processing.

Press the pastry into the bottom and halfway up the sides of a 9-inch spring form pan. Bake 6 minutes. Remove from the oven. Reduce the oven heat to 350 degrees.

To make the cheesecake:
In a medium pan, melt the 2 tablespoons butter. Add the pecan halves and toast, stirring, until barely toasted and fragrant. Remove from heat, sprinkle with 1-teaspoon fructose and toss. Set aside.

In your mixer, cream the cheese until smooth. Add the remaining ingredients and mix until just smooth. Pour the mixture into a spring form pan. Gently place the pecan halves in a circle around the outer edge of the cream cheese mixture, being careful not to press them into the batter. Continue making concentric circles with the remaining nuts. Bake the cheesecake for 1 hour at 350 degrees.

Cool in the pan. Carefully run a knife around the inside rim of the pan, then remove the sides. Chill at least 2 hours.

Serves 12.

1 slice: Total Fat (g): 42
            Protein (g): 9
            Total Carbohydrates (g): 30 (fructose); 12 (alternative sweetener)
            Dietary Fiber (g): 2
            Calories: 510 (fructose); 442 (alternative sweetener)

   Food Exchanges: Starch/Bread: ½, Lean Meat: 1, Fat: 8, Other Carb: 1½ (fructose)

Coconut Flan
Deliciously rich and creamy!

½ cup water
1½ cups fructose or agave syrup, divided
1½ cups shredded, unsweetened coconut
4 ounces cream cheese, softened
5 eggs
1 cup coconut milk
2 cups heavy cream
1 teaspoon vanilla

Preheat the oven to 375 degrees.

Before beginning, you need an 8-inch x 8-inch x 2-inch baking dish and a larger casserole into which it will fit.

In a medium saucepan, combine ½ cup water and 1-cup of the fructose over high heat. Boil, not stirring, until the liquid begins to brown and is fragrant. While boiling, you may brush the sides of the pot with a pastry brush dipped in water to prevent crystallizing on sides of pan. Be careful of heat from the steam! As soon as the sugar mixture is lightly brown, pour it into the 8 inch square baking dish. Tip the dish to distribute the mixture evenly along the bottom of the dish and slightly up the sides. Sprinkle the coconut evenly over caramelized fructose. Set into the larger casserole dish or pan.

In a large bowl, beat the eggs until thoroughly blended. Beat in the remaining ½ cup fructose, then the cream cheese. Beat until smooth. Add the coconut milk, cream, and vanilla, mixing well. Pour the mixture into the baking dish that has been coated with caramelized fructose mixture. Carefully pour water into the larger casserole, without spilling water into the flan mixture. Place into the preheated oven.

Bake 60 to 70 minutes or until the flan is soft-set in center. Remove from the oven and cool 30 minutes while still in the water. Remove from the water and cool to room temperature. Refrigerate at least 8 hours. To serve, place a large serving dish over the flan and invert. Let it set for a few minutes; then, remove the baking dish, slice into squares and serve.

Serves 10.

1 serving: Total Fat (g): 34
Protein (g): 6
Total Carbohydrates (g): 49
Dietary Fiber (g): 2
498 calories

Food Exchanges: Lean Meat: ½, Fat: 6½, Other Carb: 3

Chocolate Decadence Torte
A low-glycemic dessert especially for chocoholics.

unsweetened cocoa
4 squares unsweetened chocolate
½ cup butter
¾ cup plus 3 tablespoon fructose (or agave syrup), divided
freshly grated peel of one orange (2-3 teaspoons)
6 large eggs, separated
1 tablespoon vanilla
 whipping cream, whipped and sweetened with fructose (for garnish), optional

Preheat the oven to 250 degrees. Grease the bottom of a springform pan and line with waxed paper or parchment. Grease the pan and dust it with cocoa.

Melt the chocolate with butter in a microwave or in a double boiler, according to directions on chocolate package. Stir in the fructose and orange peel.

In large bowl, beat the egg yolks with a wire whisk. Add the vanilla. Slowly beat the warm chocolate mixture into the yolk mixture with whip, until blended.

In a small non-plastic bowl, beat the egg whites at high speed until stiff peaks form. Gently fold the egg whites into the chocolate mixture, one-third at a time.

Spoon the batter into a pan and spread evenly. Bake 1 to 1½ hours or until a knife inserted in the center almost comes out clean. The size of the pan will determine the cooking time. Cool completely.

Remove the torte from the pan and discard the parchment or waxed paper. Slice into 12 wedges. Garnish with fructose-sweetened whipping cream or serve with a small scoop of sugar-free vanilla ice cream.

Serves 12.

1 slice: Total Fat (g): 15
                  Protein (g): 4
                  Total Carbohydrates (g): 24
                  Dietary Fiber (g): 1
                  238 calories

Food Exchanges: Lean Meat: ½, Fat: 3, Other Carb: 1½

Apple Macadamia Torte

Wonderfully moist and surprisingly healthy, this torte is made with whole wheat, low-glycemic apples and healthy macadamia nuts.

1 teaspoon lime or lemon juice
1¼ cups chopped apple (about 1 large)
2 eggs
½ cup Splenda
¼ cup fructose, agave nectar, or Whey Low D
4 ounces cream cheese, softened
¼ cup whole wheat flour
2 tablespoons defatted soy flour
¼ teaspoon salt
2 teaspoons cream of tartar
1 teaspoon vanilla
1 cup chopped macadamia nuts

Preheat the oven to 325 degrees. Spray a 9-inch springform pan with non-stick spray or grease with butter. Line the bottom of the pan with parchment or waxed paper, cut to fit.

Place the lime juice in a large bowl. Peel and core the apples; then dice them into ½ to ¼ inch pieces. Add to the lime juice, and toss the apples in the juice to coat. Set aside.

With an electric mixer, beat the eggs 8 minutes on high speed. They will become thickened and fluffy. Add the sweeteners, continuing to beat the mixture. Add the softened cream cheese, continuing to beat until well blended.

While the eggs are beating, combine the flours, salt and cream of tartar. After the cream cheese is mixed in, lower the speed of the mixed to low and add the dry ingredients. Remove the beaters as soon as this is combined. Stir in the apples and nuts. Pour the mixture into the prepared springform pan.

Bake 30 minutes. Remove the torte from the oven. While it is still warm, gently run a knife along the edges of the pan to separate the sides of the torte from the pan. Open and remove the sides of the pan. Let the torte cool.

When cool, carefully invert the torte and remove the paper. Carefully turn it back over and place on your cake plate. The torte should come easily away from the bottom of the pan. If it does not, use a long spatula to run underneath the torte before removing.

Serves 12.

1 serving: Total Fat (g): 12
        Protein (g): 3
        Total Carbohydrates (g): 12
        Dietary Fiber (g): 2
        167 calories

Food Exchanges: Lean Meat: ½, Fat: 2½, Other Carb: ½

Walnut Torte
Lovely with a dollop of real whipped cream, but for a special treat,
spoon caramelized pears over the top.

¾ cups whole grain pastry flour
2 teaspoons baking powder
2 teaspoons cinnamon
4 eggs
1 cup agave nectar (or syrup)
8 ounces (1 cup) soft silken tofu
2 teaspoons vanilla
2 cups chopped walnuts

Preheat oven to 350 degrees. Spray a 10-inch springform pan with butter-flavored spray or grease with butter. Set aside.

In a medium mixing bowl, combine the flour, baking powder and cinnamon. Set aside.

Combine the eggs, agave, tofu and vanilla in a food processor until well blended. Add the walnuts and blend until the nuts are finely chopped. Pour this mixture into the bowl with the dry ingredients. Mix with a spoon just until blended. Pour into the springform pan. Bake 45 to 50 minutes, until a knife inserted in the center comes out clean. Cool at least 15 minutes. Remove the sides of the pan and serve.

Serves 12.

1 serving: Total Fat (g): 14
                Protein (g): 9
                Total Carbohydrates (g): 28
                Dietary Fiber (g): 2
                244 calories

Food Exchanges: Lean Meat: 1½, Fat: 2, Other Carb: 1

Walnut Pear Crumble

Walnut Pastry

½ cups walnuts, chopped
½ cup oat bran
½ cup soy baking mix
½ teaspoon allspice
½ teaspoon cinnamon
1/3 cup butter, softened
2 teaspoons Splenda (or granular alternative sweetener)

Preheat the oven to 400 degrees. Lightly grease an 8 inch square baking dish.

Place all ingredients except the Splenda in the bowl of a food processor, using the sharp blade. Process until the nuts are finely chopped. Remove about ¼ cup of the mixture. Add the Splenda or sweetener to this and mix with a fork. Set aside to use later.

To the mixture remaining in the processor, add 2 tablespoons of cold water. Quickly process to blend. Press the mixture into the bottom and up the sides of the baking dish.

Filling

½ cup Splenda
½ cup oat bran, divided
1 teaspoon cinnamon
¼ teaspoon nutmeg
1 cup chopped walnuts
7 cups pears, cored and sliced (about 6 large or 8 medium)
2 tablespoons lemon juice
3 tablespoons melted butter
2 tablespoons agave or fructose (or 2 tablespoons + 2 teaspoons Splenda)

In a large bowl, combine Splenda, ¼ cup oat bran, cinnamon, nutmeg and walnuts. Mix together. Add the sliced pears and toss gently to thoroughly coat the pears. Spoon into the prepared baking dish.

In a small bowl, combine the lemon juice, melted butter, sweetener and the remaining ¼ cup oat bran. Pour over the pear mixture. Crumble the reserved crust mixture over the top. Place in the oven. Reduce the oven temperature to 350 degrees. Bake 55 minutes. Best when served warm.

10 servings.

1 serving (using fructose):	Total Fat (g): 25
	Protein (g): 13
	Total Carbohydrates (g): 33
	Dietary Fiber (g): 6
	324 calories

Food Exchanges: Starch/Bread: ½, Lean Meat: 1, Fruit: 1, Fat: 4½

Coconut Cherry Pie with Almond Cookie Crust

Almond Cookie Crust
1 cup almonds pieces, finely ground
¼ teaspoon almond extract
¾ cup whole grain pastry flour
¼ cup butter, softened
2 tablespoons cold water

Combine the ground almonds with the extract. Add the pastry flour and combine. With a pastry cutter, mix in the butter until the mixture is in even-sized crumbs. Add the cold water and stir with fork. Mixture should hold together. Press the pastry evenly into a 9-inch pie pan. Bake 10 minutes at 400 degrees or until lightly browned. Set aside to cool.

Filling
¾ cup dried cherries
1 cup unsweetened coconut
1/3 cup kamut flour
2 tablespoons fructose (or alternative sweetener)
¼ teaspoon salt
2 cups plain soy milk
3 slightly beaten egg yolks
2 tablespoons butter

Meringue
3 egg whites
¼ teaspoon cream of tartar
½ teaspoon vanilla
2 tablespoons fructose (or alternative sweetener)

To make the filling,
Place the cherries in a small container and cover with boiling water. Set aside.

Combine the flour, 2 tablespoons fructose, salt, and soy milk in a saucepan. Cook and stir over medium heat until bubbly. Cook and stir 2 minutes. Remove from heat. Thoroughly drain the cherries; then stir the cherries and coconut into the mixture.

Quickly stir a small amount of the hot mixture into the beaten yolks; immediately add the yolks to the hot mixture, whisking it together. Cook 2 minutes, stirring constantly. Remove from the heat. Add the butter and vanilla. Pour into the cooled pastry crust. Set aside and make the meringue ad directed below.

Preheat the oven to 350 degrees.

To make the meringue:
Beat the egg whites and cream of tartar together in a small (non-plastic) mixing bowl until frothy. Add vanilla. Continue beating and gradually add 2 tablespoons fructose. Beat until stiff peaks have formed. Spread over the pie and seal to the edges of the crust. Bake for 10 minutes or until lightly browned. Cool on a rack.

Serves 8.

1 slice: Total Fat (g): 24
             Protein (g): 10
             Total Carbohydrates (g): 40 (fructose), 32 (alternative sweetener)
             Dietary Fiber (g): 7
             Calories: 415 (fructose), 370 (alternative sweetener)

Food Exchanges: Starch/Bread: 1, Lean Meat: 1, Fruit: 1, Fat: 4½, Other Carb: ½

Cherry Chiffon Pie with Macaroon Crust

A lovely, light tasting maroon-colored pie that's worth all the effort!
This dessert is best made the day or morning before serving.

Filling:
1/3 cup lukewarm water
2 envelopes unflavored gelatin
¼ cup lemon juice
4 cups cherries, pitted {or 2 (10-ounce) packages frozen, unsweetened, sweet cherries}
½ cup fructose or agave syrup
1 cup heavy whipping cream
2 packets Splenda
½ teaspoon vanilla

Macaroon Crust
2 egg whites
½ teaspoon vanilla
1 tablespoon + 1 teaspoon fructose (or 2 tablespoons Splenda)
½ teaspoon cream of tartar
2 cups freshly shredded, unsweetened coconut

To make the filling:
Sprinkle the gelatin into the 1/3 cup of warm water and set aside. In a medium saucepan, combine the lemon juice, cherries, and fructose. Bring just to a boil, and then reduce the heat to a simmer. Cook over medium-low heat, stirring as needed, for 30 minutes. Remove from heat and stir in the gelatin mixture. Cool to room temperature.

To make the crust:
While the cherries are cooking, preheat your oven to 300 degrees for the crust. Do not use plastic for measuring or mixing these ingredients. In a medium glass or metal bowl, beat the egg whites, vanilla, and cream of tartar until soft peaks form. Add the fructose and continue beating until the peaks are stiff (the peaks will hold their shape when you pull the beaters out). Gently fold the coconut into the egg whites, just until combined.

Spread the coconut mixture evenly over the bottom and up the sides of a deep-dish pie pan, being careful not to get the bottom too thick and spreading the mixture all the way to the top. Bake 20 to 25 minutes, just until the crust begins to brown. Remove from the oven and cool. The crust will shrink as it cools.

As the crust cools, place the whipped cream, 2 packets Splenda, and ½ teaspoon vanilla in a large bowl and beat on high until the cream is whipped. Remove the beaters, and fold in the cherry mixture gently. Spoon the cherry mixture into the macaroon crust and refrigerate at least 4 hours. Overnight is best. Serves 8 to10.

1/10 of pie:	Total Fat (g): 14	*Food Exchanges:*
	Protein (g): 4	Fruit: 2, Fat: 3, Other Carbs: 2
	Total Carbohydrates (g): 43	
	Dietary Fiber (g): 3	
	365 calories	

Pecan Fig Tart
A spicy treat for a snowy day.

1 recipe pecan pastry (following page)
2 cups dried figs, thinly sliced
2 cups pecan pieces
2 eggs, separated
½ cup fructose or agave syrup (or ¼ cup alternative sweetener)
½ teaspoon cinnamon
¼ teaspoon nutmeg
¼ cup butter, melted
2 teaspoons lemon juice

Preheat the oven to 400 degrees.

Make the pecan pastry and press into the bottom of an 11-inch tart pan. Arrange the fig slices to cover the bottom of the pastry. Set aside.

Beat the egg yolks in a large mixing bowl until thick and lemon colored. Add the fructose and spices, continuing to beat. Gradually beat in the melted butter. Stir in the pecans, mixing well.

Beat the egg whites in a small ceramic or metal bowl until stiff peaks form. Fold the egg whites into the nut mixture. Add the lemon juice while folding the egg whites into the mixture.

Pour the pecan mixture over the figs and spread into an even layer to the edges.

Bake for 10 minutes at 400 degrees. Then, reduce the oven temperature to 350 degrees and continue baking for an additional 20 minutes or until a rich, golden brown.

Cool in the pan and cut into wedges. Top with fructose sweetened whipping cream, if desired.

Serves 12.

1 slice: Total Fat (g): 27
Protein (g): 5
Total Carbohydrates (g): 44 (fructose); 32 (alternative sweetener)
Dietary Fiber (g): 7
Calories: 415 (fructose); 370 (alternative sweetener)

Food Exchanges: Starch/Bread: ½, Lean Meat: ½, Fat: 5, Other Carb: 1 (fructose)

Pecan Pastry
A delicious substitute for refined-flour pastry

1 cup pecan pieces, finely ground
¾ cup whole grain pastry flour
½ teaspoon cinnamon (optional)
¼ cup softened butter
2 tablespoons cold water

Combine the pecan pieces, flour, and cinnamon. With a pastry cutter, mix in the butter until the mixture is evenly crumbly. Add the cold water and stir with a fork. Mixture should hold together.

Press the pastry evenly in a thin layer in a tart pan or pie pan. Fill and bake.

For pre-baking, place in the oven at 400 degrees for 10 minutes or until lightly browned.

Makes 1 pastry shell.

1/8 recipe: Total Fat (g): 15
                 Protein (g): 3
                 Total Carbohydrates (g): 11
                 Dietary Fiber (g): 2
                 179 calories

Food Exchanges: Starch/Bread: ½, Lean Meat: ½, Fruit: 1½, Fat: 3, Other Carb: 1

Whipped Cream
Real whipped cream will not raise your blood sugar and is a good source of CLA.

1 cup heavy cream
2 teaspoons fructose, agave syrup, or Splenda
½ teaspoon vanilla

Put all ingredients in ceramic or metal bowl. Beat on high with electric mixer until stiff and fluffy.

Yield: 2 cups whipped cream.

2 tablespoons: Total Fat (g): 6
Protein (g): trace
Total Carbohydrates (g): 1
Dietary Fiber (g): 0
54 calories

Food Exchanges: Fat: 1

Hot Fudge Sauce

2 ½ squares unsweetened chocolate
1 teaspoon butter
1/3 cup fructose or agave syrup
1 cup heavy cream
½ teaspoon vanilla

Melt the chocolate with the butter, according to package directions.

Microwave directions: Stir the chocolate and butter together when melted. Add the fructose and mix. With a wire whisk, add the cream and mix. Microwave on high, stopping to stir every 30 seconds, until the mixture is smooth and the fructose is dissolved, about 2 minutes total cooking time. Stir in the vanilla.

Double boiler directions: Over simmering water, in the top of a double boiler, stir the chocolate and butter together. When melted, add the fructose and stir until dissolved. With a wire whisk, add the cream and stir until the mixture is smooth and creamy. Stir in the vanilla.

Serve warm over a small scoop of sugar-free ice cream.

Makes just over 1 cup.

2 tablespoons: Total Fat (g): 16
Protein (g): 2
Total Carbohydrates (g): 16 (fructose); 3 (alternative sweetener)
Dietary Fiber (g): 1
Calories: 199 (fructose); 154 (alternative sweetener)

Food Exchanges: Fat: 3½

Blueberry Crisp
Perfect with a small scoop of sugar-free ice cream.

¼ cup fructose (or 1/3 cup Splenda or other granular alternative)
5 tablespoons oat bran, divided
3 tablespoons whole wheat flour
¼ teaspoon ginger
1 teaspoon cinnamon
2 tablespoons butter
½ cup thinly sliced almonds
4 cups fresh or frozen blueberries
juice of 1 lemon

Preheat the oven to 375 degrees.

Combine fructose, 3 tablespoons oat bran, flour, ginger, and cinnamon in a small bowl and set aside.

Microwave the butter on high for 50 seconds. Add to the dry ingredients, mixing thoroughly. Mixture will be crumbly. Gently mix in the almond slices. Set aside.

Lightly grease a 9-inch glass casserole or quiche pan. Sprinkle the remaining 2 tablespoons oat bran across the bottom of the pan. Add the berries to the dish. Distribute the crumb mixture evenly over the top.

Bake 25 minutes, until the almonds begin to brown and berries are hot and bubbly.

Serve warm.

Serves 6.

1 serving: Total Fat (g): 11
        Protein (g): 4
        Total Carbohydrates (g): 22 (fructose), 9 (alternative sweetener)
        Dietary Fiber (g): 2
        Calories: 177 (fructose), 131 (alternative sweetener)

Food Exchanges: Starch/Bread: ½, Lean Meat: ½, Fruit: 1, Fat: 2, Other Carb: 1

Lemon Mousse
Light & luscious!

4 eggs, separated
2 tablespoons fresh lemon juice
2 teaspoons water
1 cup fructose, divided (half of fructose may be substituted with Splenda)
Grated zest* of 2 lemons - about 2 teaspoon
2 cups whipping cream
1 ½ teaspoons cream of tartar
1 additional lemon, thinly sliced for garnish

To sterilize the egg yolks: In a small, microwave-safe bowl, mix the egg yolks, lemon juice, and water. Cover with plastic wrap. Microwave on high until the mixture bubbles, about 45 seconds.

The mixture will look fluffy and light colored. Beat with a clean fork. Cover again. Microwave on high until it bubbles once more, about 15 seconds. Beat with <u>another clean fork</u>. As it cools, it should have the consistency of a stirred custard.

Mix ½ cup fructose and the lemon zest into the egg yolks with a fork. Set aside.

Whip the cream in a large bowl until it holds its shape and is fluffy. Fold the egg yolk mixture into the whipped cream.

In a small ceramic or metal bowl, beat the egg whites with the cream of tartar until frothy. Add the remaining ½ cup fructose; continue beating until the egg whites are stiff, holding their shape in stiff peaks.

Gently add the whipped egg whites to the whipped cream mixture, folding just until mixed.

Spoon into individual dishes or goblets. Chill several hours or more before serving. If desired, garnish each with a thin slice of lemon.

Serves 10.

1 serving: Total Fat (g): 19
              Protein (g): 3
              Total Carbohydrates (g): 31
              Dietary Fiber (g): trace
              301 calories

Food Exchanges: Lean Meat: ½, Fruit: 3½, Fat: 4½, Other Carb: 2

Key Lime Mousse: If key limes are available, substitute 2 key limes for 2 lemons.

Chocolate Chiffon Cake
Enjoy this light cake by itself or serve it up with fresh berries.

8 eggs
1½ cups whole grain pastry flour, lightly measured
1 cup Splenda
1 cup fructose, divided
2/3 cup cocoa, sifted
1 teaspoon baking soda
½ teaspoon salt
½ cup canola oil
¾ cup water
1 teaspoon vanilla extract

Preheat the oven to 350 degrees. Cut a piece of parchment or waxed paper to the shape and size of your 10-inch tube pan and line the bottom of the pan. Set aside.

Carefully separate the eggs. Place the egg whites in a large non-plastic mixing bowl and set aside. Do not refrigerate. Set the yolks aside separately in a small container.

Place the flour, Splenda, ½ cup fructose, sifted cocoa, baking soda and salt in a large mixing bowl. Combine thoroughly with a whisk.

In a medium bowl, combine the oil, egg yolks, water and vanilla extract.

Make a well in the center of the dry ingredients and pour the mixture of egg yolks, oil, water and vanilla. Beat with a whisk or electric mixer until smooth and well combined. Set aside.

Using completely clean and oil-free beaters beat the eggs whites at high speed with an electric mixer until soft peaks form. Begin adding the remaining ½ cup fructose, 2 tablespoons at a time while beating, until stiff peaks form. (Pull the beaters from the egg whites, if the peaks hold their shape and do not relax, they are stiff).

Pour the egg yolk mixture in a thin stream over the surface of the egg whites. Using a spatula or a large spoon, gently fold the chocolate-yolk mixture into the whites, just until combined. Do not over-fold. Fill the tube pan with the mixture.

Bake for 1 hour or until the cake springs back when lightly touched. Remove from oven; invert pan and cool upside-down, placing it over a bottle if necessary. Cool completely.

Remove the cake from pan when completely cool, running a knife-edge around the sides if needed. Makes a ten-inch cake (12 slices).

1 slice: Total Fat (g): 13
              Protein (g): 6
              Total Carbohydrates (g): 36
              Dietary Fiber (g): 3

Food Exchanges: 277 calories Lean Meat: ½, Fat: 2, Other Carbs: 1½

Apple Bread Pudding

Topping
1 teaspoon melted butter
¼ cup oat bran
½ teaspoon sweetener
dash ground allspice
dash ground cinnamon
½ cup chopped walnuts

Pudding
¼ cup Whey Low D, fructose or agave nectar
½ cup Splenda
3 eggs
1 cup heavy cream
1/8 teaspoon ground cinnamon
1/8 teaspoon ground allspice
½ teaspoon maple flavoring
1½ teaspoons vanilla extract
1/3 cup dried cherries, cut into raisin-sized pieces
3 slices whole grain bread, chopped or cut into ¼ inch pieces
4 tart baking apples, such as granny smith apples (about 4 cups diced)

To make the topping, melt the butter; then add oat bran, cinnamon, allspice and sweetener. Combine well. Mix with the chopped nuts and set aside.

Preheat the oven to 350 degrees.

With a wire whisk or in a mixer, beat together the sweetener with the eggs. Add the heavy cream, cinnamon, allspice, maple flavoring, vanilla, and cherries. Add the bread to mixture, stirring all together. Set aside.

Peel and core the apples, then dice into small cubes. Fold the apples into the egg mixture.

Spray a 9-inch-square ceramic or glass baking dish with a non-stick spray or grease with butter. Pour the mixture into the baking dish and press the apples flat. Sprinkle with the topping and place the dish in a larger pan. Fill the pan within ½ inch from the top with water. Cover the dessert with foil and bake 30 minutes. Remove the foil and bake an additional 50 minutes. Remove from the oven and carefully remove the dessert from the water. Let cool about 20 minutes before serving. Best when served warm.

Serves about 10.

1 serving:	Total Fat (g): 15	*Food Exchanges*:
	Protein (g): 5	Starch/Bread: ½, Lean Meat: ½, Fruit: ½, Fat: 3
	Total Carbohydrates (g): 23	
	Dietary Fiber (g): 3	
	214 calories	

Dried Fruit Cake
Be sure all fruits are free of added sugar.

2 (8 ounce) packages apricots, sliced
4 (8 ounce) packages dried cherries
4 cups (about 20 ounces) dried calamari figs, chopped (stems removed)
3 cups chopped pecans or walnuts
3 cups whole wheat flour, divided (kamut or spelt flour may be substituted)
1½ cups butter, softened
1 cup fructose or agave syrup
¾ cup Splenda or other alternative granular sweetener
6 eggs
¼ teaspoon baking soda
3 teaspoons ground cinnamon
½ teaspoon ground nutmeg
¼ teaspoon ground cloves
2 tablespoons lemon juice
1 ½ teaspoon vanilla extract

Preheat the oven to 275 degrees. Grease a 10-inch tube pan. Set aside.

Combine the first 4 ingredients; toss with 1-cup flour. Set aside.

Cream the butter in a large mixing bowl. Add the fructose and Splenda gradually, beating well. Add the eggs, one at a time, beating well after each.

Combine the remaining 2 cups flour with the spices and soda. Gradually add the flour mixture to the creamed mixture, mixing well. Stir in the fruit mixture, lemon juice, and vanilla. Spoon the batter into the tube pan. Bake at 275 degrees for 3 ½ to 4 hours or until the cake tests done (straw or wooded toothpick will come out clean when inserted in center).

If desired, bake in 3 large (9 x 5 x 2½ inch) loaf pans. Reduce the baking time to 1 hour and 45 minutes or until cake tests done as above. Cool completely in pan.

1/24 of recipe: Total Fat (g): 22
Protein (g): 7
Total Carbohydrates (g): 82
Dietary Fiber (g): 10

Food Exchanges: Starch/Bread: 1, Fruit: 3½, Non-fat milk: 0, Fat: 4, Other Carb: 1

This cake tastes best if made several weeks ahead. Brush with cherry brandy and seal in container or with plastic wrap. Brush with additional brandy at one-week intervals until served.

Strawberry Ice Cream

If you don't have time to freeze it, this recipe also makes a great batch of low carb smoothies! A scrumptious, guilt-free treat, loaded with low-glycemic strawberries.

12 ounces (1½ cups) silken tofu
1-quart fresh strawberries, about 1-1/2 cups sliced
¾ cup heavy cream
1¼ cups plain soy milk
¼ cup light agave syrup (or fructose)
½ cup Splenda
1½ teaspoons vanilla extract

Press the tofu between two paper towels to remove excess moisture.

Place all ingredients in a food processor or blender and process until smooth.

Following the manufacturer's directions, place the ice cream mixture in the ice cream freezer and freeze.

Serves 12.

1 serving: Total Fat (g): 6
                  Protein (g): 3
                  Total Carbohydrates (g): 5
                  Dietary Fiber: 1
                  114 calories

Food Exchanges: Lean Meat: ½, Fat: 1

Makes 1½ quarts (12 half-cup servings) - enough for one of today's small kitchen ice cream freezers.

Peach Ice Cream

Our favorite way to use those fabulous summer peaches! This guilt-free, high protein ice cream recipe will fool everyone. It's delightfully creamy and easy to make.

½ cup heavy cream
12 ounces (1½ cups) firm silken tofu
1½ cups plain soy milk
½ cup Splenda
¼ cup fructose
2 teaspoons vanilla extract
¼ teaspoon almond extract
½ cups fresh, ripe peaches, diced (about 2-3 peaches)

Place all ingredients <u>except the peaches</u> in a blender or food processor and blend until combined. Freeze according to directions of ice cream freezer manufacturer. Just before the ice cream is frozen, while it is still slushy, pour in the peaches and continue freezing until firm.

Makes 1½ quarts, about 10 (½ cup) servings.

1 serving:　　　Total Fat (g): 6
　　　　　　　　Protein (g): 4
　　　　　　　　Total Carbohydrates (g): 5 to 12, depending on the soy milk*
　　　　　　　　Dietary Fiber (g): 1
　　　　　　　　115 calories

Food Exchanges: Lean Meat: 1, Fat: ½

*Not all soy milks are the same. Be sure to choose one with the lowest carb count.

Perfect for today's small kitchen ice cream makers, the recipe makes 1-1/2 quarts. If you have a larger ice cream maker, just increase the recipe as needed.

Green Tea Ice Cream

Be adventurous and try this light, breezy ice cream. I like it best using plum-flavored green tea, but don't hesitate to make it with your favorite flavor!

Blackberry Sauce

2 cups blackberries, fresh or frozen
¼ cup water
1 tablespoon powdered egg whites (or 1 whole egg white)
2 tablespoons Splenda
1 tablespoon fructose

In a small pot, soften powdered egg whites in 1 tablespoon warm water; mix well to blend. Add remaining ingredients. Bring to a boil; then simmer 2-3 minutes. Remove from the heat; mash the berries; cool and refrigerate.

Ice Cream

1 cup water
10 bags green tea, fruit flavored
2½ cups heavy cream
1 cup plain soy milk
¼ cup Splenda
¼ cup fructose or agave syrup

Bring the water to a boil in a small saucepan; remove from the heat; then, add the tea bags. Cover and steep for about 30 minutes. Remove the bags, squeezing the excess fluid into pot.

In a large bowl, combine the green tea concentrate with the sweeteners until dissolved; then add all the other ingredients. Freeze according to the directions from your ice cream freezer's manufacturer.

Makes 1½ quarts, about 10 (½ cup) servings.

½ cup serving: Total Fat (g): 19
Protein (g): 2
Total Carbohydrates (g): 13

Exchanges: Fat: 3 ½, Other Carbs: 3½ (fructose)

Recipe Index

Cookies & Bars

Desserts

Dried Beans

Egg Dishes

Meat

Beef

Lamb

Pork

Veal

Nuts

Pastry

Poultry

Relish

Rice (Whole grain, of course)

Salad & Slaw

Salad Dressing

Sauces

Soup

Vegetables

Artichokes

Asparagus

Spinach

Sweet Potatoes

Tomatoes

Zucchini

Substitutions

To substitute fructose for sugar, use less fructose. For cakes, you may have to use an equivalent amount of fructose. It varies from recipe to recipe. For baking, reduce oven temperature by 25%. Baking time may increase by 5 - 10 minutes.

To substitute whole wheat, spelt, or kamut flour for white flour, reduce the amount of whole-wheat flour slightly (I start with about a 10% reduction) and increase the leavening agents (baking soda, baking powder and sometimes eggs) by 1/3 to1/2. Experimentation is the only way to be sure, but if you have favorite recipes you wish to convert, it is well worth the effort.

1 teaspoon baking powder = 1/2 teaspoon baking soda plus 1/4 teaspoon cream of tartar

1 cup sour cream = 1 cup buttermilk = 1 tablespoon vinegar or lemon juice + whole milk to = 1 cup. Let stand 5 minutes before using.

1 square unsweetened chocolate = 3 tablespoons cocoa + 1 tablespoon butter or shortening

1 tablespoon fresh herbs = 1 teaspoon dried

1 teaspoon Italian seasoning = 1/4 teaspoon each: oregano, basil, thyme, and rosemary plus a dash of cayenne

1 teaspoon pumpkin pie spice = 1/2 teaspoon cinnamon, 1/4 teaspoon ginger, and 1/8 teaspoon each: nutmeg and cloves

1 teaspoon allspice = 1/2 teaspoon ground cinnamon and 1/8 teaspoon ground cloves

1 clove garlic = 1/8 teaspoon garlic powder

1 cup whipping cream = 2 cups whipped

juice of one lemon = 3 tablespoons

grated peel of one lemon = 1 teaspoon

grated peel of one orange = 2 teaspoon

1 medium apple = 1 cup

1 medium chopped onion = 1/2 cup

1 cup canned beef or chicken bouillon = 1 bouillon (beef or chicken) cube or 1 teaspoon instant (beef or chicken) bouillon dissolved in 1 cup hot water

1/2 pound fresh mushrooms = 1 can (3 or 4 ounces) mushrooms

1/2 cup tartar sauce = 6 tablespoons mayonnaise plus 2 tablespoons pickle relish

Bibliography

Ali, R. et al. Dietary Fiber and Obesity, *Dietary Fiber in Health and Disease.* Plenum Press, 1982: pp. 139-145.

Altar, Ted, Dietary Fiber and Vegetarians. taltar@vertigo.helix.net, August 20, 1994.

Atkins, Robert C. *Dr. Atkins' New Diet Revolution.* New York, Avon Books. 1992.

Atkins, Robert C. *The Hidden Cause of Most Modern Illness and How to Defeat It!*

Allen, Ann de Wees, D.N. Effects of Sugars and Insulin on Fat Storage. *Smart Basics Intelliscope,* June 3, 1996. Smartbasics@sirius.com.

Carper, Jean. Food Your Miracle Medicine, *James Deighton's Reviews.* International Clipping Service, March 24, 1996.

Dally, Anne, et al. Tales from Carbo Land, *Diabetes Forecast,* January 1997, pp. 35-39.

Durtschi, Al, What Are Essential Fatty Acids, Anyway? *Walton Feed Presents,* mark@lis.ab.ca.

Lee, John R. *What You Doctor May Not Tell You about Menopause.* New York, Warner Books, Incup, 1996.

Mendosa, Rick. The GI Factor, mendosa@cruzio.com, Aug.9, 1996.

Mendosa, Rick and Griffin, Tere. The Glycemic Index, mendosa@cruzio.com, Sept. 24, 1996.

Menendez, C. E. and Stoecker, B.J. The Roll of the Diet in Improving Glycemic Control, *Nutrition and Diabetes,* 1985, pp.15-36.

Miller, Jennie Brand, et. al. *The G.I. Factor.* Hodder, 1996.

Netzer, Corrine T. *The Complete Book of Food Counts.* New York, Dell Publishing, 1997.

Sears, Barry, Dr. Barry Sears Zone FAQ, 1995.

Sears, Barry. *The Zone.* New York, Regan Books, 1995.

Steward, H. Leighton, et al. *Sugar Busters!* Sugar Busters, LLC, 1995.

Sugars, Insulin, Appetite and Body Fat, *Smart Basics Intelliscope*, June 3, 1996.

Printed in the United Kingdom
by Lightning Source UK Ltd.
133061UK00001B/59/A

9 781589 393035